# Academies, Free Schools and Social Justice

Academies were introduced by Labour in 2000 and first opened their doors in 2002, but during Labour's time in power the nature of the Academies changed. At first they were designed to replace existing failing schools but, by 2004, the expectation had widened to provide for entirely new schools where there was a demand for new places.

From 2010, under the coalition government, two new types of Academy were introduced. While the original Academies were based on the idea of closing poor schools and replacing them by dramatically redesigned and restructured ones, the *2010 Academies Act* allowed existing highly successful state-maintained schools to apply to become Academies as well. Further, while Labour had restricted Academy status to secondary schools, the Coalition extended it to primary and special schools. The result is that there has been a dramatic increase in the number and diversity of Academies.

In addition to this, the 2010 Act introduced Free Schools, wherein groups of parents, teachers, or other sponsors can apply to start their own state-maintained, but officially 'independent' schools. These schools can either be completely new or the result of existing private schools applying to become state-maintained. The results of these changes remain under-researched.

This book puts forward new research that examines the history and nature of Academies and Free Schools, the processes by which they have come into existence, and their effects in terms of social justice. The contributors do not all speak with one voice, but rather present a diversity of views on these important topics. Included in the collection are the results of research on pupil outcomes and socio-economic segregation; issues of identity and ethos in church academies; the problems of establishing free schools; the history of policy on Academies; and a comparison between Swedish independent schools, and Academies and Free Schools.

This book was originally published as a special issue of *Research Papers in Education*.

**Geoffrey Walford** is Emeritus Professor of Education Policy at the University of Oxford, UK.

# Academies, Free Schools and Social Justice

*Edited by*
**Geoffrey Walford**

Routledge
Taylor & Francis Group

LONDON AND NEW YORK

First published 2016
by Routledge
2 Park Square, Milton Park, Abingdon, Oxon, OX14 4RN, UK

and by Routledge
711 Third Avenue, New York, NY 10017, USA

*Routledge is an imprint of the Taylor & Francis Group, an informa business*

© 2016 Taylor & Francis

*British Library Cataloguing in Publication Data*
A catalogue record for this book is available from the British Library

ISBN 13: 978-1-138-96007-7

Typeset in Times New Roman
by RefineCatch Limited, Bungay, Suffolk

**Publisher's Note**
The publisher accepts responsibility for any inconsistencies that may have
arisen during the conversion of this book from journal articles to book chapters,
namely the possible inclusion of journal terminology.

**Disclaimer**
Every effort has been made to contact copyright holders for their permission to
reprint material in this book. The publishers would be grateful to hear from any
copyright holder who is not here acknowledged and will undertake to rectify
any errors or omissions in future editions of this book.

# Contents

# Citation Information

The chapters in this book were originally published in *Research Papers in Education*, volume 29, issue 3 (July 2014). When citing this material, please use the original page numbering for each article, as follows:

**Introduction**

*Academies, free schools and social justice*
Geoffrey Walford
*Research Papers in Education*, volume 29, issue 3 (July 2014) pp. 263–267

**Chapter 1**

*The link between Academies in England, pupil outcomes and local patterns of socio-economic segregation between schools*
Stephen Gorard
*Research Papers in Education*, volume 29, issue 3 (July 2014) pp. 268–284

**Chapter 2**

*The negotiation and articulation of identity, position and ethos in joint church academies*
Elizabeth Green
*Research Papers in Education*, volume 29, issue 3 (July 2014) pp. 285–299

**Chapter 3**

*The politics of the Academies Programme: natality and pluralism in education policy-making*
Helen M. Gunter and Ruth McGinity
*Research Papers in Education*, volume 29, issue 3 (July 2014) pp. 300–314

**Chapter 4**

*From city technology colleges to free schools: sponsoring new schools in England*
Geoffrey Walford
*Research Papers in Education*, volume 29, issue 3 (July 2014) pp. 315–329

**Chapter 5**

*Academies in England and independent schools (*fristående skolor*) in Sweden: policy, privatisation, access and segregation*
Anne West
*Research Papers in Education*, volume 29, issue 3 (July 2014) pp. 330–350

**Chapter 6**

*Setting up a free school: successful proposers' experiences*
Paul Miller, Barrie Craven and James Tooley
*Research Papers in Education*, volume 29, issue 3 (July 2014) pp. 351–371

For any permission-related enquiries please visit:
http://www.tandfonline.com/page/help/permissions

# Notes on Contributors

**Barrie Craven** is an associate at the E.G. West Centre, Newcastle University, UK. He has published several journal articles on issues in health and education economics, notably in *Applied Economics*, *Medicine, Science and the Law* and *Economics of Education Review*.

**Stephen Gorard** is Professor of Education and Public Policy at Durham University, UK. His work concerns the robust evaluation of education as a lifelong process, with a focus on issues of equity and effectiveness. He regularly gives advice to governments and other policy-makers. He is the author of nearly 1000 books and papers, including *Overcoming Disadvantage in Education* (Routledge, 2013).

**Elizabeth Green** is a Senior Lecturer and Director of the National Centre for Christian Education at Liverpool Hope University, Liverpool, UK. Her research interests include school ethos and culture, social theory and education, and Christian education. Her recent publications include *Mapping the Field* (2009), as well as a review of the most recent research on the impact of Christian education, and an article for the *British Journal of Sociology of Education* which analyses religion and education in Christian academies.

**Helen M. Gunter** is Professor of Education Policy at The Manchester Institute of Education, University of Manchester, UK. Her most recent book is *Educational Leadership and Hannah Arendt* (Routledge, 2014).

**Ruth McGinity** is a Lecturer in Educational Leadership and Policy at The Manchester Institute of Education, University of Manchester, UK. She is in the process of completing her PhD, funded by an ESRC CASE Studentship.

**Paul Miller** is a consultant at the E.G. West Centre, Newcastle University, UK. He is heavily involved in research and practice concerning application of business models to education, innovative use of technology within education, and diverse means of teacher education for optimising pupil learning. He works across a range of contexts, including within cross-cultural settings at the base of the pyramid (BoP) and in the UK. He is currently completing a doctorate concerning the use of business models for growth in low-cost private schools serving the BoP.

**James Tooley** is Professor of Education Policy at Newcastle University, UK, and director of the E.G. West Centre. He is the author of *The Beautiful Tree* (2009), a best-seller in India and winner of the 2010 Sir Antony Fisher Memorial Prize, based on his research on low-cost private education in Asia and Africa. His other books include *From Village*

*School to Global Brand* (2012), and *E.G. West: Economic Liberalism and the Role of Government in Education* (2008).

**Geoffrey Walford** is Emeritus Professor of Education Policy in the Department of Education, University of Oxford, UK. He is currently a consultant on the Open Society Foundations' Privatisation in Education Research Initiative (PERI).

**Anne West** is Professor of Education Policy in the Department of Social Policy at the London School of Economics and Political Science, London, UK. She is also director of the Education Research Group. Her research focuses on education policy, both in England and in comparative context, the financing of schools and early years education, and issues relating to equity and equality of opportunity. She has published extensively in the field of education policy.

# INTRODUCTION

## Academies, free schools and social justice

Geoffrey Walford

Academies were introduced into the English education system in 2000 by Tony Blair's Labour government as part of its *Learning and Skills Act*. They were originally called 'City Academies' and were designed to tackle social injustice by targeting children in the inner-cities where many schools were perceived to be failing. They were described as 'a radical approach' to 'breaking the cycle of under-performance and low expectations' and would replace 'seriously failing schools' which were perceived to be found in the cities (Blunket 2010). They were trumpeted as a radical innovation but, in practice, there were strong connections to previous initiatives by Conservative governments in the forms of City Technology Colleges and sponsored grant-maintained schools. Similar to City Technology Colleges, City Academies were officially independent schools, but maintained by the state and funded by central government directly rather than through local authorities. This allowed the schools to opt out of the details of the national curriculum and employ teachers on their own salary scales and terms of employment. City Academies also had sponsors who were originally expected to give £2 million towards the capital costs and who would henceforth have a controlling interest in the school. They also followed the CTCs in having a specialism, but they were no longer just restricted to technology, but could specialise in modern foreign languages, visual arts, performing arts or media arts, sport or 'any subject specified by order of the Secretary of State'.

There were further changes in the *Education Act* 2002 including the word 'City' being dropped such that these new schools became simply 'Academies' and could be established outside of cities as well. The first three Academies opened in 2002, nine more in 2003, and five more in 2004. Over the period of Labour government, the nature of Academies changed. At first, they were designed to replace existing failing schools but, by 2004, the expectation had widened to include entirely new schools where there was a demand for new places. Such Academies were not called Free Schools at this point, but they had many similarities with them as they allowed sponsors to start new schools. Later, 'successful' private schools and universities were encouraged to become sponsors and they were allowed to do so without any financial input. By the end of Tony Blair's term in office, there were 83 Academies in operation, with many more due to open in future years and a plan for 400 by 2010. Five of this total were formerly City Technology Colleges. There were greater changes when the Conservative-Liberal Coalition government took power in 2010, for they introduced two new types of Academy. Whilst the original Academies were based on the idea of closing poor schools and replacing them by dramatically redesigned and restructured ones, the *2010 Academies Act* allowed existing highly successful state-maintained schools to apply to become Academies as well. This allowed the schools to 'opt out' of local authority control in a way similar to the former grant-maintained schools, but this time, they are allowed to operate under independent school regulations which includes not having to follow the National Curriculum and having their own salary scales and working condition for staff. This first new type of Academy also does not have to find external sponsorship – indeed, many early converter schools clearly made the change in the expectation of extra funding from government. Further, whilst Labour had restricted Academy status to secondary schools, the Coalition extended it to primary and special schools. The result is that there has been a dramatic increase in the number and diversity of Academies. In August 2013, there were 3086 Academies open. This total includes several University Technical Colleges which are a special type of Academy sponsored by a local university and employers and offering technical courses and work-related learning combined with academic studies. They raise similar social justice-related questions about the selection of particular groups for certain kinds of employment that were part of the critique against CTCs back in the 1980s.

The second new type of school legislated in the 2010 Act were Free Schools which are technically a new form of Academy which clarified that Academies could be entirely new schools. Here, groups of parents, teachers or other sponsors can apply to start their own state-maintained but officially 'independent' schools. These can either be completely new schools or existing private schools can apply to become state-maintained. They cannot charge fees once they become Free Schools.

In terms of numbers, the City Technology Colleges and sponsored grant-maintained schools initiatives must be seen as failures as both schemes ended with just 15 schools. In contrast, the number of Free Schools has boomed. In the 1980s and 1990s, government support for City Technology Colleges and sponsored grant-maintained schools was rather half-hearted, but the Conservative part of the Coalition in 2010 had an election pledge to expand the Academies programme and to allow new types of school. Free Schools were seen as a major step forward in diversifying the educational system and reducing the involvement of local government in education. The central coalition government thus funded the charitable New Schools Network which was designed to help with Free school applications. Two further external factors also helped the rapid growth. First, there has been an increase in the birthrate which meant that many areas need new schools and, second, the downturn in the economy from 2008 onwards meant that many fee-paying private schools were under severe financial pressure. Not only did this mean that existing private schools threatened with closure might consider a transfer to the state sector, but also parents who might have been able to pay fees a few years earlier now considered starting their own private, but government-funded, schools.

In 2011, 24 Free Schools were opened, followed by a further 55 in 2012, and a further 93 in 2013. The range includes Steiner, Jewish, Muslim and evangelical Christian schools as well as special schools, and many Christian schools of various denominations. There is also a growing emphasis on chains of schools with sponsors of several Academies now moving into Free Schools. Some of these Free Schools are entirely new schools whilst others were existing (and usually financially failing) private schools that have moved into the government-funded sector. This increase in Free Schools is in spite of the controversy that many of them have raised and the rather mixed Ofsted school inspection reports. In August 2013, the first 24 Free school Ofsted reports were published. Four Free Schools were rated as 'outstanding', 14 as 'good', five as 'requires improvement' and one as 'inadequate'. Later, an Ofsted report on Al-Madinah Free school labelled it as dysfunctional and 'inadequate' in every category inspected (Garner 2013).

The rapid expansion of Academies and Free Schools marks a dramatic change in the way that schooling is provided in England. The local authority system of provision, funding and management of local schools, whereby democratically elected bodies plan appropriate provision for the whole local population, is being dismantled. It is being replaced by a greater diversity of provision, more completion between schools, and increased involvement of non-elected individuals and groups in the nature of local schooling. Yet, whilst these changes are fundamental to the nature of English schooling, there has been surprisingly little research published explicitly on Academies and Free Schools and their potential effects on social justice. Of course, there have been several individual articles (for example, those by Gorard (2009, 2010)), but the only book-length collection is that by Gunter (2011).

This collection of papers on Academies and Free Schools puts forward new research and scholarship that examines the history and nature of these schools, the processes by which they have come about and their effects in terms of social justice. The authors do not all speak with one voice, but present a diversity of views on these important topics.

The first paper by Stephen Gorard tackles two very important questions that need to be answered about Academies: are they more academically effective than similar non-Academy schools with equivalent pupils? Are they reducing segregation in terms of socio-economic status? It uses data from the Annual Schools Census 1989 to 2012, the Department for Education School Performance Tables 2004–2012, and the National Pupil Database and examines the national picture and the situation for local education authorities. It also gives a detailed analysis of the trajectories of the first three Academies. The article confirms earlier studies in finding no convincing evidence that Academies are any more (or less) effective than the schools they replaced or are in competition with. The prevalence of Academies in any area is strongly associated with local levels of SES segregation, and this is especially true of the more recent converter Academies. Converter Academies, on average, take far less than their fair share of disadvantaged pupils. In contrast, in line with the original intentions of the Academy programme, sponsor-led Academies tend to take more than their fair share. Gorard argues that the profiles of the two types of Academy are so different that they must no longer be lumped together for analysis as simply 'Academies'. Academies are not shown to be the cause of local SES segregation. Instead, they are merely more likely to appear in areas that already have inequitable school mixes. This means, of course, that Academies are not helping reduce segregation (as was one of their original purposes) or increase social justice in education, and the paper concludes that homogeneous maintained schools should be preferred for this purpose.

By far the largest sponsors of Academies are the Christian churches. In 2011, the Church of England had 144, and the Roman Catholic Church had 51 Academes. There are also a small number of Academies that are jointly sponsored by both churches. These are the focus of the article by Elizabeth Green. She used a case study approach to research the identity, position and ethos of jointly sponsored Church Academies, and investigated how joint church Academies are situated within the field, how they relate to existing Academies and the maintained church school sector, and how they articulate their vision and ethos. Drawing on open interviews, documentary analysis and non-participant observation, she had the unique opportunity to document the process of opening of two joint church Academies and to compare this with data from a more established joint church Academy. The research questions were the following: how do jointly sponsored Academies articulate their objectives and Christian ethos and, what is the relationship between school structures and the ethos of the academy? The article argues that joint Academies are sites of intersecting and competing fields of education, operating in relative isolation from the wider joint church school sector and from the church communities associated with predecessor schools (where applicable). Whilst sponsors used the language of 'shared values' or 'gospel values' to talk about their aims and objectives, it did not seem that the creation of joint church Academies was rooted in a robust theological framework. Potentially divisive denominational issues such as the Eucharist, collective worship and RE were discussed and resolved by the sponsors, often before senior leaders or teaching staff had been appointed. Whilst sponsors were relatively clear about their aims and Christian ethos, there were crucial points at which these objectives appeared to be lost in translation – in particular, when principals were appointed and took over the opening of the Academy and when structures such as staffing and the curriculum were put into place. Green concludes that this had the potential to dilute the distinctive aims of church education.

The article by Gunter and McGinity draws upon two of their previous research studies on Academies and investigates the politics of the Academies Programme. These two case studies examined an early City Academy that replaced two 'failing' schools, and a recent Academy that replaced a 'successful' high school. They see both of these cases as examples of a conversion process, from one type of school to another. In order to understand the process better Gunter and McGinity use some of the political tools from Hannah Arendt – in particular, the ideas of natality and pluralism – which then illuminate the depoliticisation of educational reform in England. They argue that whilst claims are made about innovation and new opportunities, there is little evidence of natality due to the Academies Programme being a conservative and neoliberal restoration project. The authors locate a failure to innovate through a denial of a range of potential options, debates and interest groups, and a notion of reform based on deferential common sense notions that elite groups know best.

Geoffrey Walford's article sets Free Schools in their historic and political context. Free Schools were announced as a dramatic way in which government policy has changed such that it is now possible for groups of parents, organisations or charities to start their own schools. They can be seen as an attempt to stimulate to 'supply side' of the quasi-market of schools but, in spite of the political rhetoric, they are far from being the first such initiative. In the long period of Conservative government from 1979 to 1987, there were two specific attempts to encourage new schools through City Technology Colleges and sponsored grant-maintained schools. Both of these initiatives stalled at just 15 schools, but it is argued that their significance was far greater than their numerical strength would indicate, and that they can be seen as forerunners of Free Schools. Whilst most commentators are prepared to see links with the CTCs, most omit to consider the sponsored grant-maintained schools as a historical parallel. The article shows that all of these schools can be seen as examples of increased privatisation and selection, and in being so they exhibit their own embedded forms of social (in)justice.

The article by Anne West presents a comparison between the Academies (and Free Schools) programme in England and independent grant-aided schools, *fristående skolor* (or *friskolor*), in Sweden. This is a particularly appropriate comparison to make as the Swedish friskolor were used explicitly as a justification for Free Schools in England at the time of the 2010 Academies Act. The paper compares and contrasts the ideological, political and legislative contexts relating to the introduction of the two programmes and the development over time under administrations of different political complexions. Two broad themes related to equality of opportunity are then explored: access to schools; and school composition and segregation with particular reference to children from different social backgrounds and those with special educational needs. It is argued that the extent to which differential school access and segregation can be attributed to the introduction of independent schools in Sweden and Academies in England is far from clear, and that it would be wrong to assume that there is a single, simple explanation.

In the next article Paul Miller, Barrie Craven and James Tooley look at the question of social justice in a different way. They argue that the Free Schools that were a major part of the Academies Act 2010 were designed to bring new people and ideas into schooling and to improve schools by responding to the needs of local communities. Their mainly empirical paper reports on the experiences of successful proposers of Free Schools through a questionnaire survey and detailed interviews with those involved with four particular schools. They show that the major motives for wishing to start a new school were the desire to improve the perceived quality of education in less affluent areas; a wish to establish a school with a different philosophy from those schools in the same area; and need to rectify a perceived local shortage of places. They report that sponsors faced several difficulties in the application process, and argue that these need to be dealt with if the process is to become more equitable and lead to greater opportunities for children.

## References

Blunket, D. 2010. *Speech to Social Market Foundation*, March 15.

Garner, R. 2013. "Michael Gove under Pressure to Tighten Monitoring as Al-Madinah Free School is Labelled 'Dysfunctional'." *Guardian*, October 17.

Gorard, S. 2009. "What are Academies the Answer to?" *Journal of Education Policy* 24 (1): 1–13.

Gorard, S. 2010. "Serious Doubts about School Effectiveness." *British Educational Research Journal* 36 (5): 735–766.

Gunter, H. M. ed. 2011. *The State and Education Policy: The Academies Programme*. London: Continuum.

# The link between Academies in England, pupil outcomes and local patterns of socio-economic segregation between schools

Stephen Gorard

*School of Education, Durham University, Durham, UK*

This paper considers the pupil intakes to Academies in England, and their attainment, based on a re-analysis of figures from the Annual Schools Census 1989–2012, the Department for Education School Performance Tables 2004–2012 and the National Pupil Database. It looks at the national picture, and the situation for Local Education Authorities, and also examines in more detail the trajectories of the three original Academies. It confirms earlier studies in finding no convincing evidence that Academies are any more (or less) effective than the schools they replaced or are in competition with. The prevalence of Academies in any area is strongly associated with local levels of SES segregation, and this is especially true of the more recent Converter Academies. Converter Academies, on average, take far less than their fair share of disadvantaged pupils. Sponsor-led Academies, on the other hand, tend to take more than their fair share. Their profiles are so different that they must no longer be lumped together for analysis as simply 'Academies'. Academies are not shown to be the cause of local SES segregation. Instead, they are merely more likely to appear in areas that already have inequitable school mixes. This means, of course, that Academies are not helping reduce segregation (as was one of their original purposes) or increase social justice in education, and the paper concludes that homogeneous Maintained schools should be preferred for this purpose.

## Introduction

Policy-makers worldwide keep creating new kinds of schools that are similar to every other kind (i.e. there is no dismantling or radical re-engineering of the concept of schools), claiming success for electoral or other reasons and then not allowing these schools to be evaluated properly. Several studies based in the US have reported evidence that attainment can be affected by the type of school attended, such as the Promise Academy charter middle school (Dobbie and Fryer 2009), Knowledge is Power Programme middle schools (Tuttle et al. 2010) and more general charter schools (Gleason et al. 2010). A recent example in England is the Academies programme, started by one government in 2000, continued by the next government from 2010 and now extended to include 'Free' schools.

City Academies were announced as a new form of secondary school for England in 2000, and the first three opened in 2002. They were independent of local authority control, like the prior city technology colleges (CTCs), and received preferential and recurrent per pupil funding, like the prior Specialist Schools. These early Academies were all replacements for existing schools deemed to be in spirals of decline, with low levels of pupil attainment, set in deprived inner city areas, losing pupil numbers and taking more than their fair share of disadvantaged pupils. They were re-badged and often re-built, with new names, new governance and management, relaxation of national curriculum requirements, and part-funded by sponsors from the private or third sectors. They were claimed by advocates to be better than their predecessor schools, in terms of pupil performance, and to be a model of a better school for the future. Over time and across political administrations in the UK, their number has grown quickly. By the time of the Schools Census in 2012, there were 1165 secondary Academies which was more than one third of all state-funded schools in England.

Originally, the Academies were set up both to stop the spiral of decline and to improve pupil results. The schools selected at the outset were among the most disadvantaged and so where they changed their intake as a result of Academisation, this was no threat to local levels of socio-economic segregation between schools. For example, where new Academies ended up taking a smaller share of local free school meal (FSM) eligible pupils, this meant that neighbouring schools had to take more and so the local clustering of poorer children into specific schools would reduce. However, the Academies programme more recently has only been driven by the purported school improvement agenda, and the social justice element is now largely ignored, meaning that almost any school is eligible to convert. Private fee-paying schools, ex-grammar schools, Foundation schools and many others (including primary) have become Academies. And the even newer Free schools have been set up as Academies from fresh. All of these are clearly nothing like the most disadvantaged schools in their area and were not in anything like a spiral of decline beforehand. This raises the very real danger of increased local SES segregation between schools, especially if the new Academies also begin to take a smaller share of FSM-eligible pupils like the early ones did.

So, this paper updates those published earlier (Gorard 2005, 2009), to address three related questions:

- What is the link between the prevalence of Academies and local levels of segregation between schools?
- Are Academies performing better than other schools, with equivalent pupils?

and so:

- Is the gain in pupil attainment from Academies worth the possible risk of increased segregation?

## Segregation matters

The issue of segregation, or clustering of similar students between schools, is an important phenomenon (Logan et al. 2012). Problems arising from the social segregation of disadvantaged students in particular schools might include damage to pupil attainment (Palardy 2013). Some studies claim that there is a school mix effect on achievement and participation, and that clustering students with similar backgrounds in schools tends to strengthen social reproduction over generations

(Massey and Fischer 2006). However, this is not well established. There are normative models showing how peers apparently become more alike, and 'frog pond' models where some students benefit from having a higher profile than their peers (Proud 2010). Others have argued that the net effect of these influences is small or even non-existent (Goldsmith 2011). There is no evidence that selective systems are better (Boliver and Swift 2011), because the overall effect is no better than zero-sum (Felouzis and Charmillot 2012).

More importantly for this paper, who attends school with who is clearly linked to longer term and wider societal outcomes. The school mix is linked to how students are treated within each school, with children in disadvantaged schools more likely to be 'diagnosed' with behavioural difficulties, whereas similar children in other schools may be labelled as having learning disabilities (McCoy, Banks, and Shevlin 2012). Classes in poorer areas have different patterns of teacher–student interaction, more like those of younger classes in more affluent areas (Harris and Williams 2012), and this can influence the achievement gap between advantaged and disadvantaged students (Knowles and Evans 2012). International studies suggest that socially segregated school systems endanger students' sense of belonging, their sense of what is fair (Gorard and Smith 2010), and may polarise information about future opportunities, by removing role models, influencing aspiration (Burgess, Wilson, and Lupton 2005) and wider social ills, such as ill health and delinquency (Clotfelter 2001). People growing up in segregated settings may then be less prepared for the academic challenges of subsequent education (Gorard and Rees 2002). Something important is being sacrificed for no apparent gain in attainment.

## Methods and sources of evidence

The questions above are addressed in this article via secondary analyses of official datasets involving all state-funded secondary schools in England other than those designated 'Special schools'.

Analysis of the intakes to schools is based on figures from the Annual Schools Census (ASC) for all mainstream state-funded schools in England from 1989 to 2012. The ASC includes the number of full-time equivalent students in each school, the number taking Free School Meals (FSMt), the number known to be eligible for Free School Meals (FSMe) and several other indicators not discussed in this paper.

The relevant intake figures for each school in each year were used to calculate the Gorard's Segregation Index (GS) at a national and local authority level. GS is the strict proportion of potentially disadvantaged students who would have to exchange schools with another student for there to be no segregation in the national school system. GS is effectively the same thing as the Hoover Index (Hoover 1941), the Delta Index (Duncan, Cuzzort, and Duncan 1961), the Women in Employment Index, the Robin Hood Index and the Student Change Index (Glenn 2011). Each school's residual for GS is the absolute value of the result of subtracting the population proportion of all students in each school from the population proportion of potentially disadvantaged students (such as those eligible for FSM) in each school. GS itself is the sum of these residuals for all schools, then divided by two. More formally,

$$\text{GS} = 0.5 \times \left( \sum |F_i/F - T_i/T| \right).$$

where $F_i$ is the number of disadvantaged children in school $i$; $T_i$ is the total number of children in school $i$; $F$ is the total number of disadvantaged children in England; $T$ is the total number of children in England.

More directly, the segregation ratio (SR) is also calculated for individual Academies. The SR gives an idea of the extent to which any school takes more or less than its 'fair share' of disadvantaged pupils. More formally, $SR = (F_i/F)/(T_i/T)$.

The Department for Education Performance Tables website (http://www.education.gov.uk/performancetables/) provides the attainment outcomes from schools for all state-funded schools in England. It includes the number of students per school at the end of their Key Stage 4 (KS4) and the figures for KS2–KS4 value-added (VA) or contextualised value-added (CVA). KS2 is the statutory assessment in core subjects usually taken at age 10 (the last year of primary school). KS4 is the assessment for age 16 + labelled 'General Certificate of Secondary Education (GCSE) and equivalent'. The VA figures include the proportion of the total KS4 students included in the measure (known as 'coverage'). VA is an estimate of the average progress made by students in each school, taking into account their prior attainment, and CVA is the same while also taking into account their background characteristics. The way the scores are calculated makes them zero-sum, and 1000 is added to the result.

The Department for Education also maintains a National Pupil Database (NPD), containing longitudinal records for all students in England including their background, SES characteristics, prior attainment, courses taken and qualifications obtained. Scatterplots were drawn for school VA or CVA estimated measures against both the number of pupils involved and the coverage of the proportion of pupils involved, in each year. Similarly, Pearson $R$ correlation coefficients were calculated for VA measures and both the number of pupils and the coverage of each school, in each year.

## Academies and SES segregation

The earliest three Academies were set up in 2002. One of these, the Business Academy Bexley, continued a pre-existing rapid reduction in the proportion of FSM-eligible children in their intake (Figure 1). The school now takes nearly half as

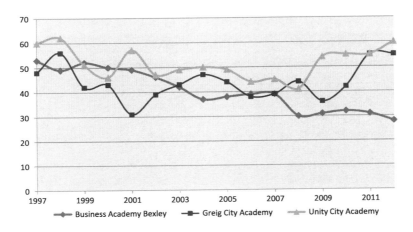

Figure 1.  Percentage of pupils eligible for FSM, first three Academies, 1997–2012.

many FSM children as its predecessor did in 1997. This change could have implications for how easy the school is to run, the barriers that the children face in attending and learning, and for the school outcomes in terms of examination results. However, in other respects not much has changed for this school. In 2002, it had a FSM SR of 2.88 meaning that it took nearly three times its fair share of FSM children. This was the highest SR in the Local Education Authorities (LEA) by some margin, and some schools had SRs as low as 0.01 (the local grammar school was taking just over 1% of its fair share of FSM children). By 2012, the SR for the Business Academy had fallen to 1.82. But this was still clearly the highest in the LEA and for much the same reasons. What seems to have happened is that the whole area has reduced levels of relative poverty over time.

The Unity City Academy in 2002 was like the one in Bexley in having the highest SR in its LEA by some margin (3.39). It took over three times its fair share of FSM children, in an area in which all school intakes had high levels of deprivation. Unity City reduced its FSM intake in absolute terms over the period 2002–2008, but the subsequent economic downturn was associated with a return to the higher levels of poverty recorded in 1997. In some ways, the situation is worse. Unity City still has the highest SR in its LEA (4.01), but this has risen to mean that the school is now taking just over four times its share of FSM pupils. Long term, neither Bexley nor Unity Academy has managed to meet one of the original objectives for these schools deemed to be in a spiral of decline, by becoming more like the other schools around it. Both are still clearly the most deprived.

As reported by Gorard (2005), Greig City Academy was never the most deprived school in its LEA and was therefore perhaps the wrong target in terms of policy at that time. In 2002, it had high levels of FSM and an SR of 2.97. However, the FSM intake of its predecessor had been falling for three years, and there were several other local schools with higher proportions of FSM. Again nothing much has changed over time. By 2012, levels of FSM were back to those of 1998, and the school had an SR of 3.67. However, this is still not the school with the most FSM children, and there are several other local schools with considerably higher proportions.

In summary, all three early Academies had a period of falling FSM following their re-badging and in parallel with their early claims to improved examination outcomes (see below). But, there has been little long-term beneficial impact on SES segregation between schools in their LEAs.

Table 1. Percentage of secondary schools within specified range of SRs, by school type, England, 2012.

| SR | All maintained | All Academies | Converter | Sponsor-led |
|---|---|---|---|---|
| <0.2 | 3 | 11 | 15 | 1 |
| <0.5 | 21 | 27 | 36 | 2 |
| <0.67 | 12 | 12 | 15 | 4 |
| 0.67–1.5 | 39 | 26 | 25 | 27 |
| >1.5 | 11 | 11 | 5 | 28 |
| >2 | 13 | 13 | 3 | 38 |
| >5 | 0 | 0 | 0 | 0 |
| N | 2095 | 1165 | 827 | 330 |

Notes: 'All Academies' include CTCs and Free Schools.
An SR of 5 is the inverse equivalent of 0.2, an SR of 2 is equivalent to 0.5, etc.

Turning to the national picture for Academies, what is clear in Table 1 is that talk of 'Academies' in general is no longer appropriate, even ignoring CTCs and the newer Free schools. Converter Academies generally take far less than their fair share of FSM pupils, while Sponsor-led Academies generally take far more than their share. They have very different profiles. For example, 51% of Converter Academies take less than half their 'fair share' of FSM pupils, whereas only 3% of Sponsor-led Academies do.

The difference between Converter and Sponsor-led Academies then manifests itself in their association with local levels of SES segregation between schools (Table 2). Whereas, in 2012, the existence of Converter Academies in any LEA was strongly positively linked to local levels of SES segregation between schools (Pearson's R of around +0.4), the existence of Sponsor-led Academies was weakly but negatively linked to SES segregation (R of around −0.15). However, LEAs with both types of Academies were linked to higher levels of segregation than LEAs with a higher proportion of Maintained schools (R of around −0.3). Before this is taken as evidence that Academies cause higher segregation, it should be noted that exactly the same pattern holds for 2002 when the first three Academies were created. And the same pattern even holds for 1999 before Academies had been conceived. It makes more sense to view the association the other way around, and state that areas with higher levels of SES segregation since 1999 are now more likely have high percentages of Academies, especially Converter Academies.

## National patterns of SES segregation

Analysis of the national patterns of SES segregation for all schools in England suggests the need for a clearer analytical distinction than previously between those factors determining the underlying level of any segregation and those affecting changes in the level over time. For example, using either take-up or eligibility for FSM, around one third of FSM pupils in England would have to exchange schools in order for all schools to have their fair share (Figure 2). For as long as records exist, and for both primary and secondary sectors, segregation by poverty has occurred at between 30 and 40%. There have been changes over time, and these changes have been identical for the primary and secondary sectors (Gorard, Hordosy, and See 2013). There is no time lag, such that secondary schools subsequently reflect the school mixes of the primary schools that feed them. Whatever it is that determines the level of between-school segregation in each year, and whatever determines the pattern of change over time, it applies to schools for both age groups of students at the same time. When school intakes become more mixed, as they did from 2008 for example, it happens to approximately the same extent in

Table 2. Correlation between percentage of each type of local school with local level of segregation, England, 1999, 2002 and 2012.

| LEA-level segregation GS FSM | Percentage of Maintained schools 2012 | Percentage of Sponsor-led Academies 2012 | Percentage of Converter Academies 2012 |
|---|---|---|---|
| 1999 | −0.31 | −0.13 | +0.38 |
| 2002 | −0.29 | −0.19 | +0.40 |
| 2012 | −0.33 | −0.14 | +0.41 |

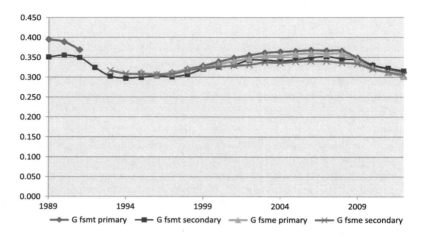

Figure 2. Levels of FSM segregation between schools in England, primary and secondary, 1989–2012.

both sectors. The same applies when school intakes become less mixed by poverty, as they did from 1998.

This result is useful, because it means that a lot of otherwise plausible explanations must be rejected. Annual changes in segregation by poverty are not caused by anything that could be specific to, or differentiated by, the age range of the schools involved. Academies have been around since 2002, and so could be involved in recent changes to segregation. But they cannot explain the pre-existing overall level of segregation. And until very recently they only affected the secondary school sector. There is no conceivable way that their onset could have created an instantaneous and equivalent change in the primary sector. Instead, the causes of the overall level must be sought in more permanent factors, while the changes over time must be linked to slower societal or economic developments, such as changes in the levels of residential segregation, which could affect both school sectors equivalently and in parallel.

Gorard, Hordosy, and See (2013) concluded that, in England, factors such as residential segregation, compounded by travel limitations and policies such as catchment areas and feeder schools, selection by ability, faith-based schools and bureaucratic boundaries are all relevant to the continuing underlying level of segregation. Smaller changes in segregation over time, on the other hand, are linked to changes in the level of that indicator in the state-funded school system as a whole. When indicators of disadvantage grow in frequency their dispersal across schools also tends to grow (creating lower levels of calculated segregation), and for FSM, this is clearly liked to the economic cycle (Cheng and Gorard 2010). For example, the level of segregation for FSM take-up 1989–2012 is correlated with the percentage of FSM students at –0.80. When the economy is good, segregation tends to be higher perhaps partly because fewer families live in poverty. When the economy falters, there is more 'equality of poverty' and levels of FSM students rise (Gorard, Taylor, and Fitz 2003). This, as above, suggests that while they are strongly associated with segregation Academies are not the main cause of either its level or variation over time. Are they better schools than their alternatives?

## Judging school performance

It is clear that attainment is strongly related to social background and prior attainment from early schooling onwards. Therefore, raw-score indicators of attainment are not a fair test of school performance. The differences in student outcomes between individual schools, and types and sectors of schools, can be almost entirely explained by the SES and prior attainment differences in their student intakes (Coleman, Hoffer, and Kilgore 1982; Gorard 2000). The larger the sample, the better the study, and the more reliable the measures involved, the higher the percentage of raw-score difference between schools that can be explained like this. However, the total variation in scores explained by student intakes will never be exactly 100%. So, the crucial question for policy is whether the small remainder of variation is merely error and bias, or whether it is evidence of differential school performance or anything else.

For a considerable time now, authors such as Goldstein (2001) have argued that this residual variation is meaningful evidence of a 'school effect', and that it can be illustrated through a valued-added approach. Goldstein and others have also argued for a long time that VA results should be used by policy-makers and practitioners to judge the performance of schools. In the VA approach, schools are judged by the progress that their students make during attendance at the school. Data on all students in the relevant school population are used to predict as accurately as possible how well each student will score in a subsequent test of attainment. Any difference between the predicted and observed test result is then used as a residual. The averaged residuals for each school are termed the school's 'effects' – and are intended to represent the amount by which students in that school progress more or less in comparison with equivalent students in other schools. A school with an average residual of zero is estimated to be 'performing' about as well as can be expected, given its intake. A school with an average above zero is doing better than expected. And this judgement should be independent of the raw-score figures, making it fairer than assessment of raw scores. Since this 'school effect' is deemed a characteristic of the school, not its students, it should be reasonably consistent over time where the staff, structures, curriculum, leadership and resources of the school remain similar over time. However, this plausible sounding approach does not work in practice for a number or reasons.

Perhaps, the biggest single problem with a VA approach is that it could never do what it was designed for – to be independent of the raw-score results. Because the VA score is based on the difference between prior and subsequent attainment, the variation in VA scores is half derived from the variation in prior attainment scores and half derived from subsequent attainment. This means that the $R$-squared correlation between prior attainment and the VA for any set of schools will be at least 0.5 (or R of above 0.7). In fact, the observed correlations can be even higher than this (Ready 2012). An example from Gorard (2006) follows.

Figure 3 shows the GCSE results in 2004 for the 124 schools with complete information in York, Leeds, East Riding of Yorkshire and North Yorkshire. The $x$-axis shows the percentage of students in each school gaining Level 2 (five or more GCSEs or equivalent at grade C or above). The $y$-axis shows the official Department for Education VA scores (with 1000 added so that 1000 becomes the average score). There is a near-linear relationship, yielding a correlation of +0.96. This means that purported VA and raw scores are here measuring what is effectively the same thing.

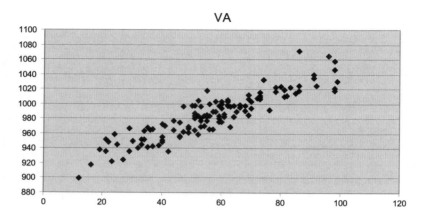

Figure 3.   The relationship between VA and absolute attainment 2004.
Source: DfES school performance tables.

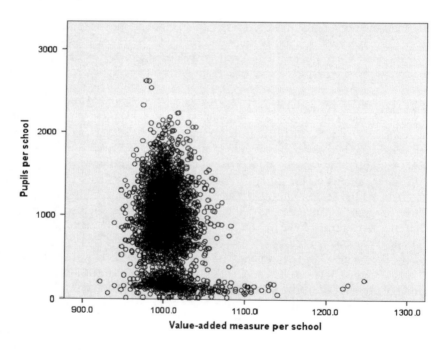

Figure 4.   Cross-plot of CVA measures and the number of students in each school, England, 2010.

VA is no more independent of subsequent attainment than prior attainment is (also correlated at +0.96). It is almost entirely predictable from the raw scores. But, these raw-score values have been rightly rejected by most commentators as not being a fair indicator of school performance.

A second problem is illustrated in Figure 4, which shows the CVA scores for all 2897 schools in England with complete CVA information for 2010. It is a cross-plot of CVA score (x-axis) and number of students in the school used to create the CVA score (y-axis). It shows that all of the very large schools have CVA at or near average, and that the most extreme CVA scores are for schools with very few pupils. This suggests that at least some of the CVA results are a consequence of the volatility of small numbers.

There is a similar correlation between coverage and CVA score (Gorard and See 2013). This means that there is a tendency for schools with less than 100% of the data for their KS4 students to appear to have more divergent CVA scores. And it is important to recall this when looking at the VA scores for Academies (below).

Due to factors like these, VA scores are much less stable than raw scores, and schools portray what are apparently dramatic swings in effectiveness every year (Kelly and Monczunski 2007). A number of studies have found VA correlations of only around 0.5 over two successive years for the same schools (Gray, Goldstein, and Thomas 2001). This is confirmed in an analysis of all secondary schools in England over five years, by Gorard, Hordosy, and Siddiqui (2013). Within two years, the clear majority of variation in schools' CVA is unrelated to their prior CVA (Table 3). Around 75% is attributable to something else. Academies are no more likely to have stable or positive CVA than other schools. This instability makes VA almost entirely useless for practical purposes, because it is not a consistent characteristic of schools and may not even be a characteristic of schools at all.

A third problem relates to error propagation. All VA analysis involves finding the difference for all students between their predicted and actual attainment. This difference will tend to be insubstantial because the model will be best fit, and the predicted and actual attainment scores will always be of the same order of magnitude. This means that the figure computed for the student VA score is usually very small, perhaps even negligible, in comparison with the attainment scores from which it is calculated. The results are also heavily dependent on the quality and completeness of the data. There will be errors and missing data in every real-life VA calculation. This creates a substantial initial source of inaccuracy for any VA calculation, and there is no way of adjusting for this statistically since the missing data are not a random subset of the data that do exist. The VA system used in England from 2006 to 2010 factored student background characteristics into the calculations. This was done in order to improve the quality of the predictions and reduce the size of the residuals for disadvantaged groups of students. This CVA sounds a sensible and fair innovation. But it means that more data are needed on each student and this adds considerably to the level of missing data. At least 10% of students are missing data every year on each key variable such as whether they are eligible for FSM, living in care and their ethnicity or additional educational needs (Gorard 2012). The outcome

Table 3. *R*-squared comparing CVA scores over time, 2006 vs. 2007–2010, England.

|  | CVA 2007 | CVA 2008 | CVA 2009 | CVA 2010 |
|---|---|---|---|---|
| CVA 2006 | 0.62 | 0.26 | 0.31 | 0.21 |

Notes: $N = 2897$ schools.
1118 of the total of 4015 secondary school or college entries on the DfE School Performance Website had significant amounts of relevant information missing in at least one year.

is a larger error component in a much smaller result. The maximum error can, and usually does, dwarf the residual by several orders of magnitude (Gorard 2010).

There is growing evidence, therefore, that for all of its appeal the VA method just does not work (Hoyle and Robinson 2003; Bradbury 2011; Ridgway and Ridgway 2011). The relevance of this is that with no evidence that individual schools are differentially effective, in terms of test outcomes at least, it follows that there is no evidence that types of schools are differentially effective, and this includes Academies.

## Academies and school performance

The earliest three Academies set up in 2002 were acclaimed an almost immediate success for reportedly achieving better results than their predecessors with equivalent pupils. These claims by politicians and the media were modified when it was pointed out that these schools no longer had equivalent pupils, and all were recording weaker examination results than their predecessor schools had for at least one recent year (Gorard 2005).

For example, the predecessor school to the Bexley Business Academy had 24% of pupils reaching Level 2 in 1998 long before Academisation, but the figure was only 21% in 2003 after becoming an Academy (Table 4). And this was despite an increase in pupil exclusions, a decrease in FSM pupils, and a national rise in GCSE results over time anyway. Until recently, its Level 2 indicator including English and Maths has also been low (in comparison to Level 2 without English and Maths), suggesting that the school has been 'playing' the system of qualification entries (see below). In 2005, the Academy recorded 15% of pupils with this tougher Level 2 indicator, while Bexley LEA schools recorded 46%. In nine recorded years, its VA measure of pupil progress for this school, as published by the DfE, has been just about as often negative as positive, and more strongly negative than positive (e.g.

Table 4.   Intake and outcomes for the Bexley Business Academy, 1997–2012.

| Business Academy | FSM | Level 2 | Level 2 including English and Maths | VA progress |
|---|---|---|---|---|
| 1997 | 53 | 13 | – | – |
| 1998 | 49 | 24 | – | – |
| 1999 | 52 | 14 | – | – |
| 2000 | 50 | 10 | – | – |
| 2001 | 49 | 17 | – | – |
| 2002 | 46 | – | – | – |
| 2003 | 42 | 21 | 15 | – |
| 2004 | 37 | 34 | 13 | 984 |
| 2005 | 38 | 29 | 15 | 972 |
| 2006 | 39 | 32 | 17 | 1004 |
| 2007 | 39 | 31 | 19 | 988 |
| 2008 | 30 | 50 | 29 | 1012 |
| 2009 | 31 | 60 | 40 | 1004 |
| 2010 | 32 | 63 | 42 | 1002 |
| 2011 | 31 | – | 52 | 991 |
| 2012 | 28 | – | 53 | 1003 |

Note: Level 2 is a government-proposed benchmark for achievement equivalent to five good GCSEs at grade A* to C, sometimes needed for entry to traditional sixth form.

984 is 16 units away from the average of 1000, whereas 1012 is only 12 units away). If believed, this is not evidence of a superior kind of school. And as already explained, the school has continuously reduced the proportion of its intake coming from families living in poverty.

The latter is important because all of the Academies that were up and running by 2005/06 took a considerably higher proportion (36%) of children eligible for FSM than the remaining educational institutions in England (13%). This is not surprising, given that they were meant to have been selected as some of the most challenged schools in the most deprived areas. It also goes some way towards explaining the generally lower level of raw-score results in Academies for students aged 16. Over the long term, national school-level results at KS4 and the percentage of students eligible for FSM correlate at around –0.5 (Pearson's $R$). Schools with more FSM students tend to have a considerably lower percentage of students reaching Level 2 at KS4. Thus, if the first thing that Academies did was to change their intakes, their outcomes should rise even if the new schools were no more effective than the schools they replaced.

As with Bexley, the predecessor to the Greig City Academy had 30% of it pupils achieve Level 2 in 2001, while only 26% achieved Level 2 in 2004 after becoming an Academy (Table 5). Again, this is despite having fewer FSM pupils in 2004 than in 1998, and in spite of the general national rise in outcome scores. In 2005, Greig City recorded 10% of pupils attaining the tougher Level 2 target including English and Maths, while the figure for Haringey LEA was 32%. By 2012, the figure for the Academy had risen to 44%, but the national figure was then 67%. In nine recorded years, its VA measure of pupil progress, as published by the DfE, has been almost as often negative as positive. None of the 'positive' results are very convincing. For example, the highest VA score for this school was in 2007, but this was calculated based on only 81% of the pupils. Any school in the country could look impressive if they could drop the least accessible or most awkward 19% of their pupils. By 2012, when the VA score was negative again, the coverage had risen to 91% of pupils (better but still far from convincing).

Table 5.  Intake and outcomes for the Greig City Academy, 1997–2012.

| Greig City Academy | FSM | Level 2 | Level 2 including English and Maths | VA progress |
|---|---|---|---|---|
| 1997 | 48 | 14 | – | – |
| 1998 | 56 | 11 | – | – |
| 1999 | 42 | 15 | – | – |
| 2000 | 43 | 25 | – | – |
| 2001 | 31 | 30 | – | – |
| 2002 | 39 | – | – | – |
| 2003 | 43 | 35 | 19 | – |
| 2004 | 47 | 26 | 10 | 983 |
| 2005 | 44 | 54 | 10 | 992 |
| 2006 | 38 | 59 | 15 | 1028 |
| 2007 | 39 | 65 | 21 | 1030 |
| 2008 | 44 | 53 | 30 | 1024 |
| 2009 | 36 | 62 | 40 | 1023 |
| 2010 | 42 | 58 | 30 | 1008 |
| 2011 | 55 | – | 37 | 996 |
| 2012 | 55 | – | 44 | 981 |

Table 6.   Intake and outcomes for the Unity City Academy, 1997–2012.

| Unity Academy | FSM | Level 2 | Level 2 including English and Maths | VA progress |
|---|---|---|---|---|
| 1997 | 60 | 13 | – | – |
| 1998 | 62 | 2 | – | – |
| 1999 | 51 | 13 | – | – |
| 2000 | 46 | 4 | – | – |
| 2001 | 57 | 17 | – | – |
| 2002 | 47 | – | – | – |
| 2003 | 49 | 16 | 7 | – |
| 2004 | 50 | 17 | 7 | 921 |
| 2005 | 49 | 16 | 6 | 908 |
| 2006 | 44 | 34 | 14 | 983 |
| 2007 | 45 | 45 | 12 | 1013 |
| 2008 | 41 | 49 | 18 | 1000 |
| 2009 | 54 | 68 | 23 | 1017 |
| 2010 | 55 | 84 | 28 | 1032 |
| 2011 | 55 | – | 25 | 998 |
| 2012 | 60 | – | 48 | 1018 |

In the year before conversion to Unity Academy, its predecessor school regis-tered 17% of pupils at Level 2 (Table 6). By 2005, three years after Academisation, the school registered 16% of pupils at Level 2. And this was with substantially fewer FSM pupils than in 2001. In 2005, the Academy had 6% of its pupils reach the Level 2 target including English and Maths, while the figure for the depressed area of Middlesbrough was 29%. Again, after becoming an Academy, this school reduced its FSM intake without any improvement in outcomes. And again, the Academy has had a mixture of positive and negative VA scores, suggesting (if school effectiveness advocates are to be believed) that it has been both a good school and a bad one, going from good to below average and back to quite good in the three years 2010–2012. In 2005, this school had one of the lowest VA scores recorded (908 or the 'inverse' of 1092). Yet, this was the year in which the Secretary of State for Education, the Specialist Schools Trust, the DfE and the BBC were all claiming that it was a success, and that Academies were a superior kind of school.

The third column in Tables 4–6 shows that where the figures overlap the situation was worse, if Level 2 requires a C grade or better in both Maths and English. This suggests that the shift in the more general Level 2 figures, above and beyond what might be expected by the reduction in FSM, is due to changes in exam entry policy. In order to boost their apparent league table position, many schools at this time began entering students for dual and triple award qualifications (such as IT), deemed to be equivalent to GCSEs, but apparently considerably easier to pass. Academies did this as well as other schools but were more secretive about their use of 'pseudo' courses, leading to calls for the Freedom of Information Act to be extended to force them to answer questions about their exam entry policies (Stewart 2010). The figures like 65% Level 2 for Greig City Academy in 2007 are likely to be based on these alternative qualifications because there is no equivalent growth of students gaining Maths and English. Subsequently, using the new official Level 2 indicator including Maths and English, neither Greig City nor Unity improved much despite a national growth in Level 2 from 48% in 2008 to 59% in 2011 and 67% in 2012. Bexley has done somewhat better than them, but not necessarily better than the national trend and has anyway continued to decrease its FSM intake. Overall, there is no clear evidence from these, or from the newer Academies, that Academies have performed better than the schools they replaced would have done (Gorard 2009).

## Conclusion

To say that struggling Academies are doing no better than their non-Academy peers or predecessors is not to denigrate them. They are doing no worse than their peers either, with equivalent pupils. Nor does it mean that good work has not been done in and by Academies. But it does demonstrate that the programme is a waste of time and energy at least in terms of this rather narrow measure of outcomes. There is no success specific to Academies that might not also have come from straightforward increased investment in 'failing' schools. Of course, one can argue that the schools have been a success in maintaining numbers and reducing the proportion of disadvantaged students. And this is certainly true for two of the first three Academies, which were selected as among the most deprived schools in England. But the programme now includes Academies that had been private or selective schools and which had been among the least deprived in their areas. So this is no longer a sensible way of assessing success for the programme. There are also opportunity costs. The money involved since 2002 could have been used differently – spent on refurbishing the most deprived schools or used to follow the most deprived students to whichever school they attend. The same is true for all recent new school schemes in England, such as the Specialist Schools, and will almost certainly be true for as yet untested schemes like Free Schools, and their equivalents worldwide.

Academies, especially the newer Converter Academies, are strongly linked to local levels of SES segregation between schools. The risk that this poses for societal cohesion and social justice is being run for no reason. The school system in England was designed through its funding, its laws about when and how school places are allocated, regulations about teacher development, inspections, National Curriculum and standard attainment in KSs, to try and make as little difference between schools as possible. England had built a system of Maintained schools that was loosely comprehensive, and funded on a per-student basis adjusted for special circumstances. The curriculum was largely similar (the national curriculum) for ages 5–14 at least, taught by nationally recognised teachers with Qualified Teacher Status, inspected by a national system and assessed by standardised tests up to KS3. Education is compulsory for all and free at the point of delivery. In a very real sense, it sounds as though it would not matter much which school a student attends, in terms of qualifications as an outcome. And this is how it ought to be, in a democratic, developed country with an education system like that in England designed to promote equality of opportunity.

The quality of education available in a national school system should not depend upon where a student lives or which school they attend. Therefore, new school types or schemes for only some schools are not the way forward. The poverty gap will be reduced by reducing differences between schools, opportunities and treatments, not by celebrating them. There should be no state-funded diversity of schooling. If, for example, Academies in England are really a superior form of school to the 'bog-standard' local comprehensives then why are only some schools made into Academies? Surely, all students are entitled to this better form of education, rather than the state wilfully continuing to provide what they claim is an inferior experience for some. In fact, it is not clear that Academies are better than other schools and so the money invested in them could have been used more fruitfully elsewhere. Again, the same could be said about most initiatives that tinker with the types of school available. For the same reason there should be no 11–16 age schools alongside 11–18 schools, or indeed any variation in age range. One of these ranges will be the better for any nation or region as a whole and should be adopted universally. If it is argued that we do not know which is best then that means we have no reason to vary them (unless for the purposes of a genuine attempt to find out). Similarly, there should be no single-sex and co-educational schools in the same system. Again, one of these forms of schooling will be better for the region as a whole and should be adopted. It means there should be no selection by aptitude or prior attainment within a system that is also compulsory. There should be no differences between schools in terms of their faith-basis, or more simply no faith-basis at all. There should be no private investment (as opposed to welcome charitable giving to the system as a whole), and no curricular specialisms in the compulsory phase (there should be a truly national curriculum). All young people should be included in mainstream institutions as far as possible. Controlling the school mix like this is one of the most important educational tasks for central and local governments.

## References

Boliver, V., and A. Swift. 2011. "Do Comprehensive Schools Reduce Social Mobility?" *British Journal of Sociology of Education* 62 (1): 89–110.

Bradbury, A. 2011. "Equity, Ethnicity and the Hidden Dangers of 'Contextual' Measures of School Performance." *Race Ethnicity and Education* 14 (3): 277–291.

Burgess, S., D. Wilson, and R. Lupton. 2005. "Parallel Lives? Ethnic Segregation in Schools and Neighbourhoods." *Urban Studies* 42 (7): 1027–1056.

Cheng, S. C., and S. Gorard. 2010. "Segregation by Poverty in Secondary Schools in England 2006–2009: A Research Note." *Journal of Education Policy* 25 (3): 415–418.

Clotfelter, C. 2001. "Are Whites Still Fleeing? Racial Patterns and Enrollment Shifts in Urban Public Schools, 1987–1996." *Journal of Policy Analysis and Management* 20 (2): 199–221.

Coleman, J., T. Hoffer, and S. Kilgore. 1982. "Cognitive Outcomes in Public and Private Schools." *Sociology of Education* 55 (2/3): 65–76.

Dobbie, W., and R. Fryer. 2009. *Are High-quality Schools Enough to Close the Achievement Gap? Evidence from a Social Experiment in Harlem.* Cambridge, MA: National Bureau of Economic Research Working Paper, 15473.

Duncan, O., R. Cuzzort, and B. Duncan. 1961. *Statistical Geography: Problems in Analyzing Area Data.* Glencoe, IL: Free Press.

Felouzis, G., and S. Charmillot. 2012. "School Tracking and Educational Inequality: A Comparison of 12 Education Systems in Switzerland." *Comparative Education* 49 (2): 181–205.

Gleason, P., M. Clark, C. Tuttle, and E. Dwoyer. 2010. *The Evaluation of Charter School Impacts: Final Report.* Washington, DC: National Center for Education Evaluation and Regional Assistance, ED510574, 259.

Glenn, W. 2011. "A Quantitative Analysis of the Increase in Public School Segregation in Delaware: 1989–2006." *Urban Education* 46 (4): 719–740.

Goldsmith, P. 2011. "Coleman Revisited: School Segregation, Peers, and Frog Ponds." *American Educational Research Journal* 48 (3): 508–535.

Goldstein, H. 2001. "Using Pupil Performance Data for Judging Schools and Teachers: Scope and Limitations." *British Educational Research Journal* 27 (4): 433–442.

Gorard, S. 2000. *Education and Social Justice.* Cardiff: University of Wales Press.

Gorard, S. 2005. "Academies as the 'Future of Schooling': Is this an Evidence-based Policy?" *Journal of Education Policy* 20 (3): 369–377.

Gorard, S. 2006. "Value-added is of Little Value." *Journal of Educational Policy* 21 (2): 233–241.

Gorard, S. 2009. "What are Academies the Answer to?" *Journal of Education Policy* 24 (1): 1–13.

Gorard, S. 2010. "Serious Doubts about School Effectiveness." *British Educational Research Journal* 36 (5): 735–766.

Gorard, S. 2012. "Who is Eligible for Free School Meals? Characterising Free School Meals as a Measure of Disadvantage in England." *British Educational Research Journal* 38 (6): 1003–1017.

Gorard, S., R. Hordosy, and B. H. See. 2013. "Narrowing Down the Determinants of Between-school Segregation: An Analysis of the Intake to All Schools in England, 1989–2011." *Journal of School Choice* 7 (2): 182–195.

Gorard, S., R. Hordosy, and N. Siddiqui. 2013. "How Stable are 'School Effects' Assessed by a Value-added Technique?" *International Education Studies* 6 (1): 1–9.

Gorard, S., and G. Rees. 2002. *Creating a Learning Society.* Bristol: Policy Press.

Gorard, S., and B. H. See. 2013. *Overcoming Disadvantage in Education.* London: Routledge.

Gorard, S., and E. Smith. 2010. *Equity in Education.* London: Palgrave.

Gorard, S., C. Taylor, and J. Fitz. 2003. *Schools, Markets and Choice Policies.* London: RoutledgeFalmer.

Gray, J., H. Goldstein, and S. Thomas. 2001. "Predicting the Future: The Role of Past Performance in Determining Trends in Institutional Effectiveness at A Level." *British Educational Research Journal* 27 (4): 39–406.

Harris, D., and J. Williams. 2012. "The Association of Classroom Interactions, Year Group and Social Class." *British Educational Research Journal* 38 (3): 373–397.

Hoover, E. 1941. "Interstate Redistribution of Population 1850–1940." *Journal of Economic History* 1: 199–205.

Hoyle, R., and J. Robinson. 2003. "League Tables and School Effectiveness: A Mathematical Model." *Proceedings of the Royal Society B: Biological Sciences* 270: 113–119.

Kelly, S., and L. Monczunski. 2007. "Overcoming the Volatility in School-level Gain Scores: A New Approach to Identifying Value Added With Cross-sectional Data." *Educational Researcher* 36 (5): 279–287.

Knowles, E., and H. Evans. 2012. *PISA 2009: How does the Social Attainment Gap in England Compare with Countries Internationally?* Research Report DFE-RR206. London: DFE.

Logan, J., E. Minca, and S. Adar. 2012. "The Geography of Inequality: Why Separate Means Unequal in American Public Schools." *Sociology of Education* 85 (3): 287–301.

Massey, D., and M. Fischer. 2006. "The Effect of Childhood Segregation on Minority Academic Performance at Selective Colleges." *Ethnic and Racial Studies* 29 (1): 1–26.

McCoy, S., J. Banks, and M. Shevlin. 2012. "School Matters: How Context Influences the Identification of Different Types of Special Educational Needs." *Irish Educational Studies* 32 (2): 119–138.

Palardy, G. 2013. "High School Socioeconomic Segregation and Student Attainment." *American Educational Research Journal* 50 (4): 714–754.

Proud, S. 2010. "Peer Effects in English Primary Schools: An IV Estimation of the Effect of a More Able Peer Group on Age 11 Examination Results." CMPO Working Paper 10/248. Bristol: CMPO.

Ready, D. 2012. "Associations between Student Achievement and Student Learning: Implications for Value-added Accountability Models." *Educational Policy* 27 (1): 92–120.

Ridgway, R., and J. Ridgway. 2011. "Crimes Against Statistical Inference." *On-line Educational Research Journal.* www.oerj.org.

Stewart, W. 2010. "Call for FOI to be Extended to Academies as Research Reveals Wide Use of 'Pseudo' Courses." *TES*, May 21, 12.

Tuttle, C., B.-R. Teh, I. Nichols-Barrer, B. Gill, and P. Gleason. 2010. *Student Characteristics and Achievement in 22 KIPP Middle Schools: Final Report.* Washington, DC: Mathematica Policy Research Inc., 116.

# The negotiation and articulation of identity, position and ethos in joint church academies

Elizabeth Green

*National Centre for Christian Education, Liverpool Hope University, Liverpool, UK*

This paper summarises the key findings of a research project into the identity, position and ethos of jointly sponsored church academies. The research sought to investigate how joint church academies are situated within the field, how they relate to existing academies and the maintained church school sector and how they articulate their vision and ethos. Using a case study approach and drawing on open interviews, documentary analysis and non-participant observation the researcher had the unique opportunity to document the process of opening two joint church academies and to compare this with data from a more established joint church academy. The research questions were: how do jointly sponsored academies articulate their objectives and Christian ethos, and what is the relationship between school structures and the ethos of the academy?

## Introduction

This paper reports findings from a research project which sought to investigate how joint church academies relate to existing academies and the state-funded church school sector and how religious communities negotiated and articulated their identity, position and ethos in three joint church academies. The research comprised an interview-based study and was carried out in three joint church academies during the academic years 2009/10 and 2010/11. This paper will briefly introduce the context of church sponsored state-funded schools in England and Wales together with the policy context of academies before exploring the existing research around joint church schools and academies. It will then account for the methodology and analytical framework of the study before presenting key findings. Little empirical research has been carried out within Christian sponsored academies and so this study contributes to our understanding of their culture and ethos and their relationship to the broader state-funded church school sector. This paper will argue that in the cases researched little attention had been paid either to the relationship of the new joint church academies to the existing academy and church school sector or to the views and aspirations of the two pre-existing communities coming together in the joint school.

## Church schools and the academies programme

The sponsorship of state-funded schools by the Church of England and Wales has been widely debated through the lens of social justice. Its persistence in the new educational landscape of academies, trust schools, federations and free schools is therefore worth examining. The debate commonly centres on the rights of parents to exercise their religious freedom vs. the rights of children to individual autonomy, the nature of religious education (RE) and worship, inclusion and religious segregation and perhaps more fundamentally whether it is legitimate for a contemporary liberal secular state to fund religious schools. Different aims and objectives have underpinned denominational conceptions of church school education. Chadwick (2012) writes that for Roman Catholics in England, schools were primarily a means of protecting the interests of a minority community 'discriminated against in a society that distrusted their loyalty to the Crown' (44). She writes that the Church of England charted a middle way looking both to the education of the nation and to the education of children in its doctrines. The relationship between different types of church school, the relationship of state-funded church schools to non-denominational state schools and the relationship between schools inside and outside of local government control have historically been an uneasy one.

The creation of academies, functioning independently of local education and enjoying greater freedoms and preferential funding arrangements is another contemporary issue largely explored in the research literature through the lenses of school choice, local democracy and social justice. The academies programme in England dates back to a Conservative government initiative of the early 1980s. City Technology Colleges (CTCs) were established in 1985 (DES 1986) to serve areas of urban social and economic deprivation. CTCs were sponsored by private business, philanthropists and Christian churches and foundations that originally had to invest two million pounds; CTCs received per capita funding but had independent school status. This model of sponsorship was adopted by the New Labour government who extended the City Academy policy as it was then known, pledging to open 400 new academies by 2010 (Gillie and Bolton 2010).

The present Coalition government continues to support the expansion of academies and their sponsorship by religious groups. The extension of the policy to include primary schools quickly increased the number of academies open. At the time that the fieldwork for this research was carried out, academic year 2011/12, there were 1419 academies open in England (DfE 2011). As of the 1st December 2012, there were 2543 academies open (DfE 2013). Scotland, Wales and Northern Ireland set their own education policy because of devolved government and they do not have academies. Every school which is rated as outstanding by the English inspection system, the Office for Standards in Education (OfSTED) may convert to academy status and these are known as 'converter' academies, new academies are known as 'sponsored'. The requirement to be in an area of low socio-economic deprivation has been dropped as has the requirement for sponsors to put in an initial financial investment. Schools judged by OfSTED to be failing may be converted into academies and run by sponsors of existing successful academies. The policy has generated fierce public and academic debate. General questions about equity, funding and the decline of the common school have been as controversial as the more specific concern about state funding for religious schools in view of a perceived rise in religious terrorism and sectarianism. This together with the sense that the landscape of education in England is undergoing considerable transition makes jointly sponsored church academies a fruitful area for considering how these relationships might manifest themselves today.

At the time of writing, there were three academies sponsored jointly by the Church of England and the Roman Catholic Church. Whilst this is a small number, there is also a small but distinct group of joint church schools within the maintained state sector who, as yet, have not taken up academy status (approx .20, source English ARC no date, accurate figures are hard to obtain since the Church of England and the Catholic Education Service list different numbers of joint church schools in their documentation). The Church of England is the largest provider of academies in England with 50 sponsored academies and 156 convertor academies; the Roman Catholic Church has 8 sponsored academies and 140 convertor academies (figures correct at January 2013, sources The Church of England and the Catholic Education Service).

To date, there has been little empirical research available in relation to academies and none published in relation to those sponsored jointly by the Roman Catholic Church and the Church of England. A number of authors write about academies at a policy level particularly in relation to the issues of democratic models for both education and social policy. Ball (2005, 2007) has written extensively about the relationship between the academies programme and what he sees as an anti-democratic re-shaping of the public sector through the participation of unaccountable modern philanthropists and businessmen. Gunter, Woods, and Woods (2009) carried out a case study of a secular academy with a specialism in business and enterprise. They used the case study to test out a typology of entrepreneurialism and have argued that traditionally individualistic business models rather than those based on collective democracy still dominate conceptions of enterprise in academies (Gunter, Woods, and Woods 2009). This author found that these models were also dominant in the CTCs and academies sponsored by non-denominational Christian foundations (Green 2009a). She suggested that Christian academies are adopting off the peg models of leadership and organisation without using their freedom to innovate as a means to critique dominant economic and utilitarian models of education (Green, 2009a). Hatcher and Jones (2006) raise questions about local democratic processes with their research into the consultation procedures surrounding the establishment of new academies. They argued that the process of creating academies fails to take seriously local opposition to the loss of their community schools and threatens parental and community rights. Hatcher (2012) has examined the response of the Labour opposition to Coalition education policies and argues that they offer no alternative vision for enhanced local democratic accountability. Gorard (2005) used the DfES own figures on school performance between 1997 and 2003/04 to contest the policy discourse that academies improve standards in education. He found that there was no evidence that CTCs and academies were performing any better than the schools they replaced.

Two research studies explore the Christian ethos and core values of academies sponsored by a non-denominational Christian foundation. Pike (2009) has investigated the relationship between the core values of the sponsor and the aspirations of pupils at Trinity Academy in Thorne near Doncaster. Trinity Academy was designated the most improved academy nationally in 2007 and is sponsored by the Emmanuel Schools Foundation (ESF). Pike (2009) concluded that the combination of business sponsorship, seven core values (honourable purpose, humility, compassion, integrity, accountability, courage and determination) and Christian ethos played a significant role in transforming opportunities for academy students. This author's ethnographic study of a CTC and two academies sponsored by ESF was the first to be carried out in the UK (Green 2009a). The study found (Green 2009a) found that although students demonstrated good biblical knowledge and valued being informed about religion, there was little evidence that the core values and Christian ethos were a strong enough vehicle to radically reshape their worldview. Whilst both Green (2009b) and Pike (2009) agree that the use of core values in the ethos creates a consensual space where different conceptions of the origins of values and morality can coalesce, this author argues that the practical effect is a dilution of the Christian basis of the ethos being communicated to students (Green 2009b). Whilst this research was not carried out in church sponsored academies, it raised pertinent questions about how ethos is perceived by students, how it is embedded or not embedded in structures, pedagogy and curriculum and whether it effectively communicates the distinctive Christian educational experience intended by sponsors. These questions overlap with those raised by Chadwick (1994) in the context of joint church schools; Chadwick's work remains the only significant research in this area and will now be briefly reviewed.

Using the story of St Bede's Joint Anglican/Roman Catholic School in Redhill where she worked as the Head of RE, Chadwick (1994) discusses a range of issues common to the creation and development of joint church schools. It is important to briefly identify these issues as they were used in the analytical framework for this study into joint church academies. Chadwick (1994) poses a number of questions which may rightly be asked of all church schools but which joint church schools have to explore from the perspectives of two traditions with their attendant concepts of parish, different theologies and different cultural norms and assumptions; all of which can create points of conflict. These questions are: how does the church school explicitly nurture the faith of its pupils, while educating them to be intellectually critical? What should be the relationship between the church school and the nearby parish communities? In what ways, if any, will the ethos or community spirit of a church school be distinguished from that of a county school? To what extent will that ethos affect the teaching of non-religious subjects in the curriculum and the way in which members of the school relate to each other (5)? Chadwick's research shows that although there are issues particularly pertinent to the joint church school context (such as if and how to celebrate Eucharist or how to teach RE in a joint church school), joint church schools also wrestle with many of the same questions that other church schools do when working out their role in an increasingly secularised society. As school communities (staff and students) become less familiar with the church and its teachings, issues around theological and spiritual literacy, what constitutes distinctive church school leadership, how to relate rightly to the expectations of parents and how to respond to the pressures of government policy become more difficult to resolve. The joint church academy research project afforded a unique opportunity to chronicle the process of creating two new joint academies and observe sponsors and senior leaders attempting to address these questions and issues; in this sense it builds directly on Chadwick's work updated for our contemporary educational context.

The next section of this paper will present the methodology of the study and demonstrate how these questions underpin the analytical framework for analysis.

## Methodology

The data collection and analysis for this research was carried out during the academic years 2009/10 and 2010/11. There were two primary research questions: (1) how do jointly sponsored academies articulate their objectives and Christian ethos? In particular how do they manage this in predecessor schools during the transition phase and (2) what is the relationship between school structures and the ethos of the (proposed) academy?

These questions were investigated through data collection in three joint church academies all of which were secondary schools (11–18 years). Two were in the process of development and officially opened in September 2011 and one had been open for over a decade. One academy amalgamated two predecessor schools, one academy replaced a Roman Catholic Church school and one academy was a new school. One of the academies was located in a large metropolitan city, the other two in provincial towns and one in a former manufacturing town; all three were located in areas of relatively low socio-economic status with a predominantly white working class population. Data were collected through documentary analysis and interview. Documentary analysis comprised documents available in the public domain such as prospectuses, consultation documents, expressions of interest from sponsors as part of the academy bid and other material which had been lodged with the Department of Education. Interviews were semi-structured, with topics and prompt questions organised around the following three themes: (i) background (this refers to context and the nature of participants' connection with the academy); (ii) sponsors and core values and (iii) transition (transition from predecessor schools where relevant). The participants comprised a purposive sample chosen because of their role in relation to the academy. These roles included: principals and vice principals, diocesan education officials, governors, representatives of management consultancy and building management companies, clergy and sponsors. In all three, academies access was gained via a letter of introduction using a known contact wherever this was possible. The interviews snowballed in that participants would recommend other people to interview and so further contacts were then followed up. A total of 15 interviews were carried out. Interviews were digitally recorded and transcribed by the researcher (this author was the sole researcher). All participants were sent a copy of the transcript and given the opportunity to amend the record if they wanted to, no amendments were made. All of the participants were over the age of 18 and able to give written informed consent, they were given written information as to the aims of the study, how the material would be used and how to withdraw; participants have the right to withdraw from the study at any point and without giving a reason. Participant data have been fully anonymised but due to the small size of the sample, it may be possible to identify the academies themselves even though they are not named in any writing about the research. As a result, Academies are not reported on individually in this research and participants were informed that this would be the case. The gender of participants is not given in this paper nor their specific job title in order to further protect their anonymity, selected quotations from transcripts have been used to provide supporting evidence of key findings but summaries in the author's words are also used where it is necessary to protect anonymity. A delay of at least two years has been built in to the publication of this research so that no material appeared at the same time as the new academies opened.

## Analytical framework

The analytical framework used for analysis in this research draws on an approach modelled by Grace (2002) in his research into Catholic school mission in the context of the marketisation and secularisation of the English education system and further developed by this author in relation to Christian sponsored academies (see Green 2012). Grace framed a set of theoretical questions using Bourdieu's concepts of field, habitus, capital and symbolic power to investigate what forms of capital leaders in Catholic schools may draw on in the contested field of Catholic education.

Bourdieu's social analysis assumes that being situated in culture regulates our assumptions, relationships and values and reproduces them in our social practice (Bourdieu and Passeron 1977). Bourdieu used the concept of field to define the dimensions of the social space, so for example a system of education would operate as a field. Grace (2002) would describe Catholic education as a field. This illustrates an important point about the concept of field, which is that different fields in the social world overlap; so Catholic education in England overlaps with the field of state-funded education. In this study, Catholic education also overlaps with Anglican education, a field that Chadwick argues (1994, 1997, 2012) is traditionally regarded as less cohesive or tightly bounded and this will be discussed in relation to the data below. This overlap creates competition within fields arising from different assumptions about what education is for and manifesting itself in competition for position and cultural recognition.

Habitus refers to our deeply rooted assumptions, not explicitly reflected upon but held almost subconsciously, which stem from our worldview. There is a lot of discussion in the literature about whether Bourdieu equated habitus with ethos and it is beyond the scope of this paper to fully explore this (see Smith 2003, for further discussion), however the concept of habitus within Bourdieu's work is very much connected with the idea of worldview particularly in the context of religion. Rey (2004) writes that Bourdieu understood the religious habitus to be 'the specifically religious dimension of an individual agent's habitus that manifests itself most apparently, though not exclusively, in the religious field' (337).

Bourdieu argued that the acquisition of cultural capital primarily through the social institution of education can confer distinction upon an individual and therefore material advantage (Bourdieu and Passeron 1977, proposition 3.1.3, 35). Symbolic power refers to the power that can be exercised by those groups in society who have more cultural capital. This power is often exercised institutionally via social structures such as education or religion. In Bourdieu's framework the concept of symbolic power is used to track the exercise of power within an institution and explores how certain practices are recognised and legitimated to validate and control the accumulation of cultural capital within the field.

In this study, Bourdieu's concepts have been used in tandem with the questions that Chadwick (1994) posed in relation to church schools to frame a set of analytical questions with which to interrogate the data. A full list of questions can be found in the endnote to this paper but are broadly grouped as follows: (i) questions for structural analysis, including questions like do joint academies constitute a 'field' or are two separate fields in operation (Catholic and Anglican), if so what is the relationship; (ii) theological questions, such as what theological understanding underpins concepts of education and ethos and (iii) Church school questions, these comprised the questions posed by Chadwick and an additional question: what is the relationship of academies to the dual system? The key findings of the research are discussed below.

## Key findings

This paper presents three intersecting findings from the joint church academies research project: First, joint church academies are sites of intersecting and competing fields of education; second, they are relatively isolated from other joint church schools; and third, there is considerable potential for the aims of the church sponsors to be diluted at critical points in the creation of a new academy. Joint church academies as sites of intersecting and competing fields will be discussed first and then the isolation from other institutions and the dilution of sponsors' aims will be considered.

## Joint church academies as sites of intersecting and competing fields

Ball (1990) has written about the ways in which national policies are interpreted and often reinterpreted at a local level. The greater the number of stakeholders involved, the greater the potential is for competing understandings of the nature and purpose of education. Whilst academies are designed to be independent, innovative and relatively free from the politics of local education provision, the number of sponsors involved, complex consultation processes and stringent levels of national accountability may in fact create a very complex web of competing interests (see Ball 2005; Hatcher and Jones 2006). With respect to the joint church academies, these interests may be grouped under the following headings: denominational, socio-economic and political. Discussion in this paper primarily focuses on competing denominational interests and will seek to illustrate how these are overlaid with perspectives that stem from class or from status and positioning e.g. clergy and laity.

All three of the academies in the research sample had multiple sponsors. In addition to the Church of England and the Roman Catholic Church, this included a variety of organisations such as universities, and other independent schools. All three of the schools were located in areas of relatively low social and economic status where middle-class parents educated their children predominantly out of area. One academy in the research sample was a new school and two others replaced predecessor schools, admissions arrangements were complex and did not necessarily replicate the catchments of previous church schools or overlap with parish boundaries. There had not previously been a Church of England secondary school in any of the sample locations. This means that from the perspective of at least two local communities, their local non-denominational school had been closed and replaced with a church school. In both of those instances, there was also some opposition from Catholic parents to the perceived loss of 'their' Catholic school and this is an important theme to explore further as an example of competing denominational interests in the field overlaid with social, economic and political factors.

Where links with distinct local communities constituted geographically, or in the case of church schools denominationally, are diluted by the closure of a local school, we might expect that the nature of the community in the new academy takes on even more significance. The research found that for some participants, expectations of how the denominational character of the school would explicitly manifest itself ran high and in all three sites the voice of the Catholic community, lay and clerical, was more clearly discernible than that of the Church of England. Grace's (2002) work around 'catholicity' and the historic legacy of Catholic schools being closely connected to their respective communities helps to account for the strong current of feelings associated with the closure of predecessor Catholic schools in this sample; but so too does the social-economic context and political (with a small p) identity of the communities involved. Bourdieu's conceptual tools help to reveal the inter-play between religious beliefs/assumptions and those associated with class and regional identity. Participants who lived and worked in the areas surrounding the predecessor schools pointed out that they constituted relatively insular communities. In one instance, a Catholic school served a pocket of lower socio-economic status bounded by very wealthy communities in the rest of the town. The school roll had been fall-ing and one Catholic participant articulated some frustration that wealthier Catholic families tended to educate their children out of area. There remained a strong per-ception that the Catholic school served the poorer community and hadn't received the proper credit or support for hanging in there and offering a Catholic education to local Catholic families.

From the perspective of diocesan officials, Catholic places in all three locations needed to be secured in the context of falling rolls regardless of whether places were offered in a Roman Catholic school or a joint Catholic and Church of England school. One of these interpretations is not necessarily right and the other wrong, the point is that they co-existed as narratives within the same space and they illustrate competing assumptions about the nature and purpose of religious faith and educa-tion. One of the dividing lines is undoubtedly denominational. In all three sites, par-ticipants who identified as Catholic expressed some uncertainty about how the Church of England understands its educational mission and ethos, in some cases this was expressed as outright scepticism. There was an assumption that Catholic educa-tion was somehow stronger with a more clearly understood vision. Of even more interest was that this view was articulated by both Catholic and Church of England participants. For example, one Anglican participant described the presence of the two churches in one location as follows:

> The Catholic church is very evident and powerful and structured, the Anglican Church less so. But of course there's a weighting factor in that because the Catholic Church was strongly connected through [name of predecessor school removed to preserve ano-nymity]. And of course what this gave rise to as we moved forward into consultations was that the Catholic Church were better mobilised. And what really did emerge was, I don't know what you'd call it really, vicarious religiosity … the Anglicans were new on the block in that sense, and our structures and processes were less well formed.

> [Interview Transcript, I2]

From the perspective of the sponsors, it seemed that Anglican participants in the research acknowledged that *The Way Ahead* (2001) review had asserted a clearer vision for distinctive Anglican schooling but also felt that joint church academies could benefit from the clarity of purpose and structural power associated with existing forms of Catholic education.

In both of the locations where a new academy replaced a Catholic predecessor school, the local opposition from Catholic parents was interpreted by Anglican participants as having more to do with class than religion. One participant argued that local parents whose children attended a community school:

were so thrilled by the fact their kids were going to have the opportunity to be in a new school they weren't worried about the fact that it was going to be a church school. They just wanted their children to have a chance. But the Catholic parents were very outspoken and the bottom line was they didn't want their kids mixing with [name of community school removed to preserve anonymity] kids.

[Interview Transcript, I1]

This research project did not interview parents and so the validity of this interpretation cannot be established; it has been included as an example of where the competing perspectives lie and how issues of religion and class intersect. It illustrates the positioning of 'other' denominational groups in the field as the problem and it may also reflect misconceptions on the part of other participants about how Catholic parents understand the place of the school in their parish community.

Another line that intersects with denominational difference in the field is the distinction between Catholic clergy and laity. Those members of the clergy who were interviewed regarded parents and students as part of the community of the church whereas lay participants pointed out that many families were un-churched and saw the community of the joint academy as distinct from that of the church. One Catholic lay participant reflecting on his experience of working with the Church of England for the first time in the creation of a new joint church Academy felt that the Church of England was more realistic about this and summed it up as follows:

This is just what I got from the Church of England whereby there's no assumption that they [pupils] will necessarily have been churched ... So even though they're coming to a, you know, it's not a joint faith, a Church of England school it's a recognition of where they're starting from, you know in terms of any journey that they have. Now I think with Catholic, you've got your primary schools. It's still, I suppose, how can one put it, there's still hope that people would have gone to a church, should be churched. And it's more 'they've never been to church isn't that awful' sort of approach rather than an acceptance of young people's lives or family life today and what the nature of the mission is.

[Interview Transcript, I7]

The point here is not to argue that Church of England schools are better attuned to the needs of an un-churched pupil population; rather this is evidence of the existence of different perspectives regarding the purpose of education and the nature of the community in a church school which all have to find a way to co-exist in a joint church academy. In this particular instance, it is interesting that working with a different denomination enabled this participant to articulate a level of frustration with the approach of some Catholic clergy and to be confronted with different ways of representing the community of the school. Having identified this arena of denominational struggle, the key question is to what extent is a new cultural understanding (Bourdieu would call this 'habitus') being formed in the site, how is this negotiated, who are the key spokespersons i.e. where does the power lie in the construction of ethos? To link this to the questions that Chadwick (1994) poses: in what ways, if any, will the ethos or spirit of the joint church academy be distinguished from its predecessor school(s)? These questions will be explored further as we discuss the relationship of joint church academies to joint church schools, to the local church communities and the articulation of sponsors' aims.

## Isolation from other institutions and the dilution of sponsors' aims

Using Chadwick's (1994) research as a point of comparison, the study found that all three joint church academies had faced a very similar set of issues to those encountered by St Bede's Redhill as it was established. Bringing two church communities together for worship, wrestling with identity as a church school, and deciding on an RE curriculum are all identified by Chadwick (1994) as potentially divisive issues that joint church schools routinely face. Due to the lack of empirical research in this area, it is not clear whether they are resolved in similar ways across the joint church school sector. They were not addressed in the same ways in the three joint church academies. Two out of the three joint church academies had decided not to celebrate joint Eucharist in order to side step an issue deemed too controversial to tackle in their particular diocesan context. In one of these academies attendance at services in the chapel was voluntary; the chapel was a tiny room tucked away to the rear of the building and not the kind of focal point often found in church schools. In all three joint church academies, the RE curriculum had been an issue of significant concern for Catholic parents and sponsors. Catholic sponsors had been adamant that RE should have 10% of curriculum time; one participant explained that not achieving this would have been deal breaker in the creation of one of the academies:

> I think if we'd said well actually it's only going to be 9.5% I think the whole thing would have gone into halt.

> [Interview Transcript, I4]

In her work, Chadwick (1994) acknowledges that resolving potentially contentious issues around worship, religious identity and RE can be painful but argues that in order for partnership between denominational groups to be real and meaningful they need to be openly discussed with the whole community before decisions are reached. Furthermore, she argues that these kinds of discussions are a significant part of the process for bringing two church communities together and becoming secure in their identity. A participant involved in the opening of two joint church academies explained how important it had been for the sponsors to work together to drive through their vision. When asked how issues of disagreement had been handled, this participant seemed to think it was better that such challenges be resolved by sponsors and if necessary dealt with behind closed doors:

> there were different ideas around the table but at the end everyone wanted to achieve the same thing and I think these sponsors are the same and I think that is part of the journey that they've had … working together I think things get ironed out in the end and get sorted out.

> [Interview Transcript, I3]

This contrasts with the experience Chadwick (1994) writes about at St Bede's where the staff from the amalgamating schools were encouraged by the head teacher to meet regularly in departments and working parties to discuss all aspects of schools life and to report to on what their contribution could be. Well-attended staff prayer meetings continued weekly for up to two years at St Bede's after the joint church school opened. A significant area of difference for the joint church academies of course is that they were opening as new schools. In one case, the previous school, and by association its staff, was deemed by OfSTED to be failing, furthermore the failing school was the non-denominational school; leaving the Catholic predecessor identified in the community as the stronger academic partner. The institutions were going through a stressful regulatory process called Transfer of Undertakings (Protection of Employment) (TUPE) which protects employee's terms and conditions when a business is transferred to a new owner (ACAS 2013). When asked to comment on whether staff had been consulted and included in discussions about the new academy, its ethos, its curriculum and its new building, one participant argued that this was difficult to do this without raising people's expectations around what their own jobs might be. It was considered important by participants that the joint church academies be seen as completely new schools and that, what were perceived as, poor teaching practices and low standards were not simply transferred across:

> you do want to consult with staff and engage with them but that's also tricky because things will be different in the new academy, people might not be in the same role that they're in now when they transfer across … And we're going to start coming to a tricky part now with starting the TUPE process because I'm not sure if some staff realise that and I'm wondering if some staff just think yeah, I'll transfer across and I'll just do what I do now – which defeats the object of the Academy.

[Interview Transcript, J3]

This is potentially one of the critical areas where the aims of the sponsors carefully written into the education brief and other planning documents may not be passed on to the wider community. The process of tackling potentially divisive issues and taking a position on the nature of worship, RE and determining the core values of the ethos in the joint church academies happened separately from the appointment of staff and often before the recruitment of principals and senior leaders.

What is interesting is that although these issues have also been contentious for other joint church schools, the research found no evidence that sponsors had talked to the governors or diocesan teams involved in their creation. There had been some consultation with other academies and a sharing of experienced personnel, local authority and diocesan expertise during the planning stages. For example, participants who held posts in other established academies served on committees or offered advice, but the bulk of their contribution was to areas not considered 'religious' such as legal matters, finance and project management. The prevailing view was that the joint church school identity and Christian ethos was really a matter for the sponsors. This is partly explained by the fact that the academy policy has deliberately created a sector which does not have to operate in relation to other schools outside of Academy chains or federations. Government policy does actively encourage sponsors to take on chains of academies and to build on their experience of running them but this author has argued that this encourages the uncritical duplication of existing structures and operating processes (Green 2009a). This author also argued that academy models were very hierarchical with top down systems of decision-making and she found that this was also compounded by a theological hierarchy (Green 2009a). In other words, staff who shared the religious background of the sponsors were more visible in the academies both in relation to decision-making processes but also as spokespersons for the Christian ethos (Green 2009a).

In one of the locations in the sample, there was a considerable history of the Roman Catholic and Church of England dioceses working together in partnership. It was not possible to thoroughly examine the theological frameworks written into the education briefs for the joint academies in the sample since they were not all publically available. Analysis of the interviews carried out with key participants who had been involved in writing the briefs and closely involved in the bid process for the two new academies suggested that the framework largely relied on the language of 'shared values' and articulated a commitment to be faithful to both traditions and welcoming to those of 'other faiths and none'. Some participants talked about the importance of sharing 'gospel values' and contributing to the mission of the church. The majority of the participants interviewed were frustratingly vague about the theological basis for the mission and ethos in the joint church academy that they were involved in. The exception to this were two Catholic participants who were able to clearly articulate a theology of Catholic education but who were very frustrated with the experience of working on the creation of a joint church academy, 12 months later they were no longer working on the project. The wider research literature around church schools in England suggests that school leaders lack theological literacy and are not confident about articulating the ethos and mission of their schools in these terms (see Green and Cooling 2009). One of the participants argued that appointing a head teacher and leadership team to take ownership of the sponsors' ethos and to mobilise it in the institution was a critical point at which a sponsor's mission and ethos might be diluted:

> The question for academies ... is who is the guardian of the mission? Is the mission clearly identified? Is it owned is it checked on Is it in the heart of the pace or is it in the mind of one person? So I've seen academies I have to say produce great responses but along comes the head teacher: I'm going to do it this way. That's the autonomy of the profession.

[Interview Transcript, I2]

This reflects contemporary discourse in which school leaders, in particular principals, shoulder almost sole responsibility for the success or otherwise of their schools. Within the academy model principals effectively function as Chief Executive Officers. In a church academy, let alone a joint church academy, this places considerable trust in their ability to lead a faith community and yet this will have been addressed only briefly, if at all, in their training. With the caveat that a detailed analysis of the education briefs has not been carried out, the findings from this research suggest that a clear theological rationale for the distinctive identity of a joint church school may not have been handed on to senior leadership teams in the first place. The rhetoric around Christian ethos in the documentation of the academies researched often portrayed a community built around a shared set of values but in practice sponsors assumed that ethos could be 'created' in the new school using a top down delivery model. This model is often dependent on explicit ethos statements, teaching in RE and assemblies and in the pastoral care structure (Green 2009b). Donnelly (2000) describes this as a positivist model arguing that rather the true nature of a school ethos needs to be researched in the gap between what is imposed top down and what is generated from the bottom up. This author's research in this gap found that structures and processes, curriculum and pedagogy communicate ethos to students often more powerfully than explicit teaching about Christian values in RE and collective worship (Green 2009a). Chadwick's (1994), Donnelly (2000) and Green's (2009a) research all suggest that ethos is not something that can be worked out in advance and handed on. If a joint church school ethos is best formed through negotiation within a community, as Chadwick (1994) argues, then the approach taken by the joint church academies in this study would appear to be flawed.

## Conclusion

This research project sought to investigate how joint church academies are situated within the field, how they relate to existing academies and the maintained joint church school sector and how they articulate their vision and ethos. It found that joint academies are sites of intersecting and competing fields of education, operating in relative isolation from the wider joint church school sector and from the church communities associated with predecessor schools (where applicable). Whilst sponsors used the language of 'shared values' or 'gospel values' to talk about their aims and objectives, it did not seem that the creation of joint church academies was rooted in a robust theological framework. Potentially divisive denominational issues such as the Eucharist, collective worship and RE were discussed and resolved by the sponsors, often before senior leaders or teaching staff had been appointed. This contrasts with the nature of collaborative working recommended by Chadwick (1994) as an essential component of establishing a joint church school committed to meaningful partnership between denominational communities. The research concluded that this approach had the potential to dilute the distinctive aims of joint church school education.

## References

ACAS. 2013. "Transfer of Undertakings (TUPE)." Accessed January 4. http://www.acas. org.uk/index.aspx?articleid=1655

Ball, S. J. 1990. *Politics and Policy Making in Education: Explorations in Policy Sociology*. London: Routledge.

Ball, S. J. 2005. "Radical Policies, Progressive Modernisation and Deepening Democracy: The Academies Programme in Action." *Forum* 47 (2): 215–222.

Ball, S. J. 2007. *Education plc: Understanding Private Sector Participation in Public Sector Education*. London: Routledge.

Bourdieu, P., and J.-C. Passeron. 1977. *Reproduction in Education, Society and Culture*. London: Sage. (Re-published 1990).

Chadwick, P. 1994. *Schools of Reconciliation: Issues in Joint Roman Catholic Anglican Education*. London: Cassell.

Chadwick, P. 1997. *Shifting Alliances: Church & State in English Education*. London: Cassell.

Chadwick, P. 2012. "Conflict and Consensus in the Dual System." In *Anglican Church School Education: Moving Beyond the First Two Hundred Years*, edited by H. Worsley, 43–60. London: Bloomsbury.

Dearing, R. 2001. "The Way Ahead: Church of England Schools in the New Millennium." The National Society for Promoting Religious Education. Accessed August 17, 2012. http://www.churchofengland.org/media/1234378/gs1646.pdf

DES. 1986. *A New Choice of School*. London: HMSO.
DfE. 2011. "Faith Schools: Faith Academies." Accessed May 14. http://www.educa-tion.gov.uk/b0066996/faith-schools/faith.html
DfE. 2013. "Open Academies and Academy Projects in Development." Accessed January 8. http://www.education.gov.uk/schools/leadership/typesofschools/academies/b00208569/open-academies.html
Donnelly, C. 2000. "In Pursuit of School Ethos." *British Journal of Educational Studies* 48 (2): 134–154.
English ARC. "2013 Joint Anglican-Roman Catholic Schools." Accessed January 1. http://www.cte.org.uk/Articles/190991/Churches_Together_in/Working_Together/Theology/Dialogues/English_ARC/Joint_Anglican_Roman.aspx
Gillie, C., and P. Bolton. 2010. *Academies Bill Research Paper*. London: HMSO.
Gorard, S. 2005. "Academies as the 'Future of Schooling': Is This an Evidence-based Policy?" *Journal of Education Policy* 20 (3): 369–377.
Grace, G. 2002. *Catholic Schools: Missions, Markets and Morality*. London: RoutledgeFalmer.
Green, E. 2009a. "An Ethnographic Study of a CTC with a Bible-based Ethos." DPhil thesis, University of Oxford.
Green, E. 2009b. "Speaking in Parables: The Responses of Students to a Bible-based Ethos in a Christian City Technology College." *Cambridge Journal of Education* 39 (4): 443–456.
Green, E. 2012. "Analysing Religion and Education in Christian Academies." *British Journal of Sociology of Education* 33 (3): 391–407.
Green, E., and T. Cooling. 2009. *Mapping the Field: A Review of the Current Research Evidence on the Impact of Schools with a Christian Ethos*. London: Theos.
Gunter, H., P. A. Woods, and G. J. Woods. 2009. "Testing a Typology of Enterpreneuralism: Emerging Findings from an Academy with an Enterprise Specialism." *Management in Education* 23 (3): 125–129.
Hatcher, R. 2012. "Gove's Offensive and the Failure of Labour's Response." *Forum* 54 (1): 29–36.
Hatcher, R., and K. Jones. 2006. "Researching Resistance: Campaigns Against Academies in England." *British Journal of Educational Studies* 54 (3): 329–351.
Pike, M. A. 2009. "The Emmanuel Schools Foundation: Sponsoring and Leading Transformation at England's Most Improved Academy." *Management in Education* 23 (3): 139–143.
Rey, T. 2004. "Marketing the Goods of Salvation: Bourdieu on Religion." *Religion* 34 (4): 331–343.
Smith, E. 2003. "Ethos, Habitus and Situation for Learning: An Ecology." *British Journal of Sociology of Education* 24 (4): 463–470.

## Appendix 1. Analytical questions

*Questions for structural analysis*

Do joint academies constitute a 'field' or are two separate fields in operation (Catholic education and CofE education), if so what is the relationship?
What assumptions do actors from different fields bring with them? What are the different tastes and dispositions?
What are the hierarchies?
Are strategic decisions and institutional structures entirely new? What assumptions are embedded in them?
What are the arenas of struggle?
How does a long run-in time or a short one relate to embedding assumptions?

*Habitus*
Is a new habitus being formed? How is it being created, through crisis, imposition?
Which old beliefs persist? NB sub-consciously held, not necessarily reflected on thus might draw on ideological, theological, pragmatic conditioning.

Is geographical location and historical context significant and are these co-dependent? Significance of local and national trends.

*Symbolic power*
What are the symbolically powerful relationships? Who is the spokesperson? Are these traditional or different? What is intentionally being constructed? What will impact practice?

*Cultural capital*
What has value? How are valued networks constructed, who is part of them? What has currency? What are the dominant discourses for Academies, faith academies in particular? Is building and architecture symbolic?
Is there a relationship between class and ecumenism?

*Theological questions*
Do leaders speak in terms of faith formation?
What theological wells do leaders draw on?
What theological understanding underpins concept of education and ethos?
Do different theological approaches compliment, co-exist, conflict, dominate?
Where is religion in this space? Relationship to the marginalisation of religion (Chadwick, 1994, 5).
How is worship and word manifest?
Is there a common view of Christian education within an Anglican and RC context?

*Church school questions*
What is the relationship of academies to the dual system?
*Questions posed by* Chadwick (1994)
How does the Christian school explicitly nurture the faith of its pupils, while educating them to be intellectually critical? What should be the relationship between the Christian school and the nearby parish communities?
In what ways, if any, will the ethos or community spirit of a Christian school be distinguished from that of a county school?
To what extent with that ethos affect the teaching of non-religious subjects in the curriculum and the way in which members of the school relate to each other? (5).

# The politics of the Academies Programme: natality and pluralism in education policy-making

Helen M. Gunter and Ruth McGinity

*The Manchester Institute of Education, University of Manchester, Manchester, UK*

Our investigations into the politics of the Academies Programme in England have generated thinking that draws on data about the conversion process from two projects. We engage with an early City Academy that replaced two 'failing' schools, and a recent Academy that replaced a 'successful' high school. We deploy Hannah Arendt's political tools of natality and pluralism to illuminate the depoliticisation of educational reform in England. We identify that, while claims are made about innovation and new opportunities, there is little evidence of natality due to the Academies Programme as a conservative and neoliberal restoration project. Integral to this is the urgency of reform based on deferential common sense notions that elite groups know best. The denial of a plurality of options, debates and interest groups in the conversion process is delivered by co-opted educational professionals as reform managers.

## Introduction

Political debates, policy manoeuvres and legislative reforms regarding publicly funded education in England have been about the imagining, promotion and realisation of the 'independent' school as the preferred model. The provision of educational services as local schools interconnected within a system governed through individual school governing bodies, area-based local authorities (LAs) and elected councils, and a national UK government department and Parliament has been variously challenged, reformed and is in the process of being dismantled. Schools with governing bodies in England, and under the direction of the national UK government, have been restructured as 'independent' of the LA and elected councils in three main ways: first, the establishment of new provision outside of the LA. e.g. City Technology Colleges from the mid-1980s, and Free Schools from 2010; second, the removal of schools from the LA, e.g. Grant Maintained Status from 1988, and Academies from 2000; and third, major interventions into LA provision such as Fresh Start from 1997 (where a school closed and then reopened with new staffing), and the National Challenge from 2008 (where a framework for improvement was imposed on selected schools deemed at risk and National Challenge Advisers were appointed to support the school and the LA). The notion of 'independence' is based on removing the school from local democratic accountability by building on the self-managing school as a business in a competitive market place created through the Education Reform Act of 1988. The language is one of 'specialisation' and 'choice', where 'diversity' of provision would enable 'standards' to improve. Consequently, such 'independence' has warranted further changes whereby Academies and Free Schools can operate outside of national workforce conditions of service and the national curriculum, and have facilitated the dominance of powerful interests (e.g. faith groups, businesses, and individual philanthropists). The shift from a predominantly public 'system' to private 'provision' is not yet settled or complete but there are visible trends through the promotion of parental choice, the shift of public assets into private hands, the outsourcing of provision to private interests, and the discourses around 'for-profit' educational services, interplayed with localised compliance and development of 'independence' schemes.

Within this context, our contribution is to report on thinking that asks serious questions about the political processes regarding securing 'independence' located in the Academies Programme. Specifically we site our intellectual work in the politics of 'conversion' for two Academies, the first is the creation of a City Academy in the early post-2000 period through the closure of two predecessor LA schools, and the second is the change by a LA school into an Academy under the terms of the 2010 Act. The argument we intend making is based on mobilising Arendt's analysis of the political process, and in particular her work on pluralism and natality. Specifically, we focus on 'conversion' as a key aspect of 'academisation' where we make the case that 'conversion' is more about labour and work than about political action, and by deploying her thinking about natality and pluralism, we illuminate a failure to be innovative through the denial of a range of potential options, debates and interest groups who have something to contribute to developing educational opportunities.

## What's new?

The launch of the Academies Programme in 2000 was located in a fanfare of doing something dramatically different in order to make significant and necessary improvements to the provision of education in urban areas. Blunkett (2000) stated that 'for too long, too many children have been failed by poorly performing schools which have served to reinforce inequality of opportunity and disadvantage' (unpaged), where the solution was to invest in new forms of schooling, and so 'City Academies will create opportunities for business, the voluntary sector and central and local government to work together to break this cycle and improve the life chances of inner city children' (unpaged). Blunkett was speaking as Secretary of State for Education on behalf of the New Labour government that had taken office in 1997 with a commitment to 'put behind us the old arguments that have bedevilled education in this country' and they had proposed 'Fresh Start' schools where a failing school would close in the July and reopen in the September (New Labour 1997, unpaged). By the time of the 2001 election, this policy had not brought about the improvements expected of it, with high profile cases of head teacher resignations in the press (Gunter 2005). So the *Ambitions for Britain* manifesto (New Labour 2001) stated that: 'New Labour believes that schools need a step change in reform to make quality education open to all' (unpaged) and central to this was a commitment to diversity. A range of initiatives were announced, regarding the growth in specialist schools and the need for more church schools, and with a clear stake in the 'new City Academies' (unpaged) that had begun to roll out: '… we will establish more City Academies, and promote greater innovation in the supply of new schools with local consultation. We will allow greater involvement in schools by outside organisations with a serious contribution to make to raising standards ...' (unpaged). The Academies Programme that had begun with the City Academies from 2000 developed incrementally over the decade from its inception and the change of government in 2010 generated continuity and expansion (Gunter 2011). The Coalition agreement in 2010 stated that they would create 'new Technical Academies as part of our plans to diversify schools pro-vision' (HM Government 2010, 29), and went on to radically expand the programme, not least through the inclusion of primaries and successful secondary schools. When combined with the plan to allow 'Free Schools' where 'new providers can enter the state system in response to parental demand' (HM Government 2010, 28), then the idea of the state-of-the-art independent school, funded by the tax payer but run by private interests, became the main focus of reform.

Our study of the politics of the Academies Programme from 2000 (Gunter 2011, McGinity and Gunter 2012, forthcoming) suggests that election campaigns and the operationalising of the mandate to govern through major restructuring and reculturing were based on a perceived need to enable something new to happen in the provision of educational services. The New Labour lexicon around the Academies Programme was dominated by the words 'innovation' and 'freedom', and this became central to how those who were actively involved framed their personal, symbolic, political and economic investments. Those who have written about their experiences do so on the basis of frustrations with the existing system, and the opportunities that 'new freedoms' were promising for the profession and local communities (see Astle and Ryan 2008, Daniels 2011, Leo, Galloway, and Hearne 2010). Hence, the academies were 'free' from the national curriculum, did not have to accept national workforce terms and conditions of service and could experiment with the curriculum and organisational arrangements. Sponsors could invest funds (up to £2 million in the original scheme), and increasingly their know-how and standing either as individuals or as established groups (e.g. faith organisations) could help break with the 'bureaucracy' of local government and the 'stranglehold' of trade unions, and the 'cultures of depression' that they are said to have generated (see House of Commons 2009). From 2010, there has been a shift from a 'some-thing must be done about inner city schools' towards a 'something must be done about all schools' where it is claimed that those who are doing well within LAs can do even better outside. So schools that are officially failing remain prime candidates for academy status, but the approach has increasingly been more about creating the conditions in which academy status is an obvious move for the successful school. There is an energy and drive to enable all schools to be restructured as autonomous, as Gove (2012) has stated:

> Labour's Academies Programme proved genuinely transformative and provided a solid basis for our reforms. But we had more than just the evidence of history to lean on. The principle of autonomy-driven improvement is solidly backed by rigorous interna-tional evidence. The best academic studies clearly demonstrate the effect of empower-ing the frontline. Trust professionals and they will exceed your expectations. (unpaged)

Within this context schools are going through a process of academisation from LA-maintained school to an independent state school, and it is the political processes involved that we intend thinking about.

## Conversion

Academisation of schools in England has been aspirational whereby Blair (Northampton Academy n.d.) imagined a time when all schools would be academies, and an emerging reality whereby Gilbert et al. (2013) talk about 'an increasingly academised system' (5), and declare that 'academisation is one of the most significant structural transformations' (9). Academisation is used to describe a range of changes that are indeed structural, where Courtney (2013) has mapped the current rapidly unfolding school landscape and identified at least 80 types. For the purposes of this paper, we are acknowledging the current situation for academies that are 'sponsored', 'convertor' and 'enforced sponsored' (Gilbert et al. 2013, 16). These labels denote the interplay between a school being forced to change (sponsored, enforced sponsored) and seeking to change (convertor), and hence, the process is not just a legal one in regard to the status of the school (including funding and governance), but is also about the wider political matters regarding how a school comes to go through the process. Academisation is about closing a school and reopening an academy, it is therefore about cultural and professional change, and speaks about identity issues that impact on the practice of teaching and learning.

Within this context, we intend using the term 'conversion' to illuminate a particular part of academisation, and in deploying it, we intend to give meaning to the Academies Programme from 2000 rather than accept the government use of the term for current 'convertor' academies. This is a helpful way of developing understandings because conversion embraces a process designed to be revolutionary, and in ways that are not just about the technical legalities of a change for one particular type of academy but are about how people think about and practise such a change across the system. There are new dispositions to be cultivated, new ways of organising learning, and new people to be embraced in the organisational and governance structures. Literally, people have to be converted to the idea and the realities of academies as both 'independent' and 'state' schools, and so the inter-relationship between those who hold public office and those in civil society who are located within the conversion process needs to be taken into consideration. Hence, in the first phase of city academies teachers, children, and parents had to be converted to the idea that an independent school would resolve the failings of the current schools in their locality; whereas in the current phase of post-2010 'convertor' schools, teachers, children, and parents had to be converted to the idea that high standards within the LA can be guaranteed outside of the LA.

This process is necessarily political in the sense that as Blunkett and Gove illustrate (see above) there is a need to present and sustain a case for change in ways that will speak to all those directly involved from parents, to teachers, to sponsors and to children. In this sense, the imperative for academisation to take place is based on a form of 'preaching' in oral and written texts (e.g. see DfE 2010), and how it is received is integral to whether those in receipt are receptive as 'converts'. While research evidence (e.g. Wrigley and Kalambouka 2013), commissioned evaluations (e.g. PwC 2008), and Parliamentary scrutiny (e.g. NAO 2007) have all raised serious questions and presented challenging evidence about the Programme, not least that there is no evidence of 'an academies effect' (PwC 2008), politicians of the left and right have remained resilient in their promotion of the independent school and have been able to generate a sense of normality (Gilbert et al. 2013). Hence, conversion is not just about academisation *per se* but about the opportunities to gain advantage in the market place for those who ordinarily cannot afford fees for private education. This is a necessary process for strategising towards for-profit provision, with the return of vouchers as a means through which purchasing can be extended to low-income families.

Research has been done on forms of resistance (see Gunter 2011, 2014) and the Anti-Academies Alliance remains robust in challenging conversion strategies and tactics. This opposition is helpful in enabling understandings that conversion is about how the purposes of 'public' schools and schooling is not settled, and who is involved in the design and development of the curriculum, pedagogy and the workforce is broader and more influential than under the previous LA and professional groups. Hence, the process is one of both radical futuring and adaptation on ground, where major changes in the organisation and funding of schools is taking place to create improved provision which has had to be translated into local policies and practice. This requires at least acceptance and hopefully enthusiasm from all those involved. In many ways, the spiritual sense of conversion is also appropriate as new ways of thinking and doing as professionals, children and parents are required as a salvation narrative (see Gunter 2011, 2014). Conversion requires a break with the past, particularly by fracturing and restorying individual and collective memories. Reactions to national and local resistance to conversion illustrate this, where politicians have sought to denounce those who are working to retain their schools within LA control and/or for different models of local provision.

We present two illustrations of this conversion process where we do not report on fieldwork and data *per se,* but use our learning from this to develop an approach to thinking. The first story is located in the setting up of Metropolitan City Academy opened in the first tranche of academies from 2000, whereby two schools were closed in order to create the Academy. This is a *forced conversion* whereby sponsors were recruited and required to fund and take ownership of the school and the standards of education (see Gunter 2011). The story is based on a research project funded by the British Academy where Gunter was co-investigator and a member of the fieldwork team. The case study began during the conversion process and continued through the first two years of the Academy's existence. Data-sets were collected from children, teachers, senior leaders, sponsors, other schools in the area, and the local authority, and for this paper, we refer to, but do not directly report on, data-sets developed from fieldwork with the head teachers of the predecessor schools, and from the principal and senior leaders of Metropolitan City Academy.

The second story is located in the transition of Kingswood High School into Kingswood Academy following the 2010 Academies Act. This is a *convertor academy* whereby the school decided to apply for academy status and sponsors have been invited to work with the school. The story is based on a research project funded by the ESRC as a doctoral CASE studentship, and was a case study of localised policy-making with McGinity undertaking the role of doctoral student as an 'embedded' or researcher in residence. The doctoral project focused on the development of learning cultures and practices from 2010 through to 2013, and during the period the school underwent the conversion to an Academy. Data-sets were collected from children, parents, teachers, senior leaders, governors, and for this paper, we refer to, but do not directly report on, data-sets developed from fieldwork with the principal and senior leaders.

## Story 1 – preaching to convert

As Metropolitan City Academy was in the first phase of the Academies Programme, it was under the spotlight not least in regard to improving student outcomes through testing. While the two predecessor High Schools were closed down at the end of a school year, and the Metropolitan City Academy was opened with a new Principal, workforce, curriculum, and with a state-of-the-art new building planned, the whole process was highly contested. The aim for those who initiated and generated the plan was to locate a radical approach to new schooling in the area of the city within a major regeneration project regarding housing and the economy. The original plan for an academy fell through due to the withdrawal of a sponsor having faced opposition and threats. Indeed, the community opposed the formulation of the Metropolitan City Academy plan, due to concerns over the land where the new building would be located, and cultural antipathy between the two communities that supported the predecessor schools. The data show the importance of the sponsors in rescuing and promoting the Academies project in this area of the city, with a commitment to investing in the community as a means of both 'giving something back' and to benefitting their own concerns. Emphasis was put on the separation of the sponsors from the newly appointed professionals, but at the same time, the importance of both supporting and challenging in order to bring about improvements. The networks that these sponsors were located within were seen as beneficial to aspirations regarding entrepreneurialism and to accessing resources to realise these aspirations.

In summary, the politics of the conversion process shows the following:

Sponsors: they drove the conversion process and had a hands-on role in the appointment of the Principal and Senior Leaders, the organisation of the school and the curriculum. Importantly, they brought business techniques and culture to the curriculum and the organisation, and gave the workforce access to resources and networks that would support this process.

Principal and senior leadership: they drove the educational vision and the setting up of the organisation. Importantly, they accepted business techniques and culture in the design and delivery of the curriculum and the organisation.

Workforce: they are a combination of staff appointed from the two predecessor schools and new staff, and overall they were more positive than negative, with claims made that the culture was more focused on innovation with the resources to do things. But with concerns over the role of business, and with one respondent claiming that the predecessor school where they had worked had not been failing.

Children: activity in the new Academy showed overt compliance through everyday processes, but the data show concern regarding the lack of authentic involvement in the decision to close their predecessor schools, and their lack of support for aspects of the new curriculum.

Parents: while their children were attending the Academy, the data show opposition from within the community, this focused on community distinctiveness as well as concern regarding the location of the new building.

The data show that overall the conversion process was one of 'preaching' as a means of 'converting' those who had to recognise how the change being done to them was integral to economic regeneration for the area. The opportunities for the staff were presented as a form of professionalisation, whereby doing something different was a mantra for improvement. A culture of negativity towards the heads of the predecessor schools, the local authority, and the local community is a strong feature, with a language of 'war', 'battlefields', 'survival' being used in the accounts given of the reasons for and the experience of the conversion. Such a process was highly stressful and there is much evidence of unpleasantness and threats (both verbal and written) towards those managing the conversion. Data from the predecessor school heads show a concern that their schools were not 'failing' (with evidence supplied of improvements), but remained in need of investment and revitalisation, with heads of other local schools and the LA identifying problems regarding local planning and co-ordination, not least with enrolment and transfer.

## *Story 2 – preaching to the converted*

Kingswood High School was closed in 2012 and in order for Kingswood Academy to open a legal conversion process had to be gone through. The transition was visible through a branding, and new investment in the buildings and curriculum. The aim was to build on the success of the school in a highly affluent area through generating improved opportunities for learning, particularly in regard to business and vocational training. The school had a history of innovation and had engaged with successive reforms through developing original interpretations regarding localised policy-making. For example, the application for specialised school status in the early part of last decade was based on a rejection of specialisation between schools and in favour of specialisation within the school. The argument was that as a comprehensive school it did not make sense for the whole school to specialise in one curriculum area (e.g. languages, sport, business, technology), but it did make sense to personalise the curriculum through enabling the children to exercise choice regarding how they wanted to design their learning. The success of this proposal created a positive approach in regard to the handling of centralised reforms locally. Consequently, the response to the 2010 Academies Act was based on a view that the full academisation of the system was inevitable, and so the school should get on board and make it work before they were forced to convert. Kingswood did not have to convert in the way that the two predecessor schools to the Metropolitan City Academy had been forced to close, and indeed, Kingswood had developed forms of independence from the LA that had been productive. It seems that the spaces and opportunities for autonomy within the LA system had created the conditions and dispositions to leave it.

In summary the politics of the conversion process shows the following:

Sponsors: they had been approached and brought on board by the school leadership, and have been involved in curriculum design and accreditation, and have given the workforce access to resources and networks that would support this process.

Principal and senior leadership: while they remain troubled by the Academies Programme, they originated and drove the decision and built commitment within the school and community. Importantly, they have a negative view of the local authority and have led on the importance of building business sponsorship with the concomitant techniques and culture.

Workforce: they are highly supportive of the school and have accepted the principal and senior leadership decision about the necessity for and vitality of the conversion.

Children: they are highly supportive of the school and where there are concerns they are about issues that the school knows about and is working on.

Parents: they are highly supportive of the school and want to enable it to provide the best education possible. The town has large discrepancies in socio-economic status of families, with a buoyant private sector, and so in the longer term, the issue will be about how parents may move from private to state independent education, how current private schools may convert as competitor state independent schools, and how parents may set up a competitor free school.

The data show that overall, the conversion process is one of 'preaching' to the 'converted' or at least to those who would not overtly challenge what was being presented as an opportunity for curriculum innovation. The school has used its own research to investigate curriculum and whole school issues as a means of enabling development, not least through asking questions about whether children and families are expected to fit the school culture and how the school can know and understand family and community aspirations better. The Academy conversion at Kingswood has not been based on its own local research but on an acceptance of the current national policy discourse combined with the sidelining of concerns about what this might mean for the inclusion policy as a comprehensive school serving the whole community. It seems that their success so far in handling national policies locally, in ways that bring the school local gains, has generated a confidence that they can put their unease to one side. The shift to 'school-led school improvement' (DfE 2013, unpaged) has been embraced, though as yet the Academy has not been asked to support improvement in another school in ways that could potentially enhance or endanger its own position, and it has not yet faced competition from a 'free school' as new provision. Interestingly, while there are examples of schools in other regions of England grouping together with the LA to plan and develop education locally, this school has not done this. They had recognised that the Department would not do business with a school within a LA, not least because the 'comprehensive' school had become a toxic brand, and so there was a need to do something to enable the school to retain the gains made over the past decade in localised policy-making. It seems that 'going it alone' has been an audacious feature in the localised enactment of major policies such as specialisation and academies, and it is enabling the school to stake novel branded claims in a locally competitive market.

These two sites of conversion raise questions about the polity and the processes by which national education policy is working through in localised policy processes. Importantly, the projects speak to Apple's (1993) identification of an 'official knowledge' that is communicated through a 'politics of common sense' (1), whereby the neoliberalism of entrepreneurial sponsors and the neoconservativism of faith sponsors confirm the crisis in public education and provide solutions that strengthen their interests (see Woods, Woods, and Gunter 2007). Fabricated urgency combined with a 'there is no alternative' to academies is based on a liberation narrative, which interlinks with traditional professional values of doing your best for the children, or at least getting hold of a reform and making it work in ways that prevent too much damage. A crisis was created for both schools where the solution was located outside of LA accountability processes: Metropolitan City Academy was based on a centralised compulsion to break the LA monopoly, and Kingswood Academy was based on an acceptance of a centralised compulsion that the LA monopoly is an anachronism. Consequently, local policy-making is about professionals being converted into reform managers, or more accurately how successive reforms have created ways of working that have generated opportunities for elite professionals, where building commitment with teachers, children and parents enables neoliberal and neoconservative projects to be realised.

## The politics of conversion

We have presented conversion as a wider and more enveloping process than that suggested by the 'convertor' label under the 2010 Act. Following Arendt (2005), we would want to examine the politics of conversion in ways that not only challenge what has and is taking place, but also enable us to think about ourselves as researchers. This is important because while we have some accounts of conversion (e.g. Barker 2010, Elliott 2011, Hatcher 2011), there is little that examines the political processes *per se*.

While much might be said about current disappointments and even revulsion with politics, we would want to associate with Stoker's (2006) claims about how and why politics matters, because it:

> ... can provide a means of getting on with your fellow human beings that aims to find a way forward through reconciliation and compromise without recourse to straightforward coercion or outright violence. It provides a way to live in an ordered manner with your neighbours, but one that unavoidably often calls on you to sign up to deals and compromises that might not be your first or even tenth choice, but which nevertheless have something in them that enables you to put up with them. It might not be very inspiring, but when it works politics delivers one great benefit: it enables you to choose, within constraints, the life you want without fear of physical coercion and violence being used against you. Politics creates space for human choices and diverse lifestyles. Politics, if done well, creates the positive context and stable environment for you to live your life. That's why politics matters. (7)

Such an approach to politics is based on opportunities and space through which options and decisions might take place, and where debates and thoughtful choices might be public. It is out of the scope of this paper to engage with evidence and discourses about the precious nature of the public domain, but we would want to confirm the diversity of publics (Newman and Clarke 2009) and how the current anti-political culture is putting this at risk (Marquand 2004). In Scott's (1998) terms, hierarchy continues to work through political processes whereby complex ideas are communicated as 'simplifications' as a means of enabling 'legibility' (77) by those in receipt of them. Illustrative of this are the claims about sponsors, who it is argued 'challenge traditional thinking' and who 'seek to make a complete break with cultures of low aspiration' (DCSF 2009, unpaged). These types of simplifications do not interconnect with historical evidence about the creativity of LAs, and that schools have been and are successful under Local Authority control. This is about 'seeing like a state' in ways that are not 'simple minded' but is about using facts in ways that are 'replicable across many cases' (81). So seemingly different interests in the Academies Programme (e.g. politicians, civil servants, business, professionals, faith groups) can associate together through a predisposition to exercising power and legitimacy through hierarchy. Indeed, the know-how, the experience, the leadership of sponsors has been characterised in ways that legitimise forms of oligarchy (see SSAT 2007, 9). While seemingly pluralistic political processes are taking place (e.g. elections, manifestos, TV debates), in reality it is 'simplification, abstraction, and standardisation' (81) that dominates. The practical knowledge and knowing of children, parents, and professionals is messy, incoherent and can be easily condemned as unmodern and unhelpful. In this climate, the silences are loud, whereby people who are in the midst of it can be caught up in the discourse and may be prevented from raising their concerns. Our argument is that politics is being taken out of educational choices about purposes and practices, not just through the dominance of a convergence of neoliberal and neoconservative ideologies, but because the elite interests that are dominant are enabled to opt out. They inhabit a world where they may not have children or their children do not go to the schools that they claim to be investing in. When they opt into practical matters, it is being a presence (see SSAT 2007, 90), or through working with and supporting the principal and governing body. It is about building markets for their ideas (faith groups) and products (entrepreneurs), and securing a 'compliant ready' workforce and citizenry. How the Academies Programme illustrates this process of depoliticisation of public education can be understood through Arendt's political tools and analysis regarding what she describes as action.

There is much activity around academies but little action. By this, we mean that people are committed and busy in the creation and establishment of the idea and reality of academies. In Arendt's (1958) terms, this activity is mainly a form of labour and work, where the former is about survival (eating, warmth), and the latter is about crafting something (artefacts, ideas) that are durable and can outlive our mortality. In this sense, our two examples are about people who want schools to survive within particular contexts, and so make this happen through the practice of making academies work. Academies have been laboured over rather than created, and without action, there is no politics with a space to share, debate, and decide. There are two aspects to this: natality and pluralism.

Natality is about how birth generates the capacity for something new:

> Labour and work, as well as action, are also rooted in natality in so far as they have the task to provide and preserve the world for, to foresee and reckon with, the constant influx of newcomers who are born into the world as strangers. However, of the three, action has the closest connection with the human condition of natality; the new beginning inherent in birth can make itself felt in the world only because the newcomer possesses the capacity of beginning something anew, that is, of acting. In this sense of initiative, an element of action, and therefore of natality, is inherent in all human activities. Moreover, since action is the political activity par excellence, natality, and not mortality, may be the central category of political, as distinguished from metaphysical, thought. (Arendt 1958, 9)

Education is integral for natality, and so the teacher's role is crucial in doing what Arendt calls 'preserving newness' (Levinson 2001, 14). This is challenging as there is a need to create learning in ways that open up possibilities for something different but within the context of threats to natality, not least through how particular versions of history are deployed. This is why the involvement of teachers in the politics of change is vital, because Arendt ascribes to them the need to take and exercise responsibility for learning. However, while the Academies Programme is replete with the language of newness and an urgency to do something new, there is little that is new. Replacing the LA with autonomous academies or linked academies as a 'chain' is about transferring rather than replacing the logic of control. Our examples show that it is a conservative restoration project whereby elite interests are imposing their model of the independent school that is not independent by virtue of their economic, cultural and legal control. And even though various types of schools fail to deliver (e.g. Academies, Grant Maintained, City Technology Colleges, Free Schools) the idea of independence has remained remarkably uncontaminated, but is reinvented through a process of forgetting. Consequently, children are denied natality because the curriculum and ways of doing things are repackaging and rebranding control structures. In both of the example Academies, the work-related curriculum is being devised in ways that segregate children, with the re-emergence of the grammar and secondary modern schools 'by the back door'. What is most shocking is how those who are concerned about the bigger picture of the Academies Programme are complicit with it, and spend time convincing others that they should also be accepting – on the basis that things will be better, without considering better for whom. Arendt is helpful here through her analysis of pluralism as being integral to action, and policy analysis reveals a denial of other ideas and imaginings that extends beyond the Academies Programme (Gunter 2014).

Arendt (2005) argues that: 'politics is based on the fact of human plurality. God created *man*, but *men* are a human' (93), and so: 'politics arises *between men*, and so quite outside of man … politics arises in what lies between men and is established as relationships' (95). Elite interests in the formal political process (e.g. political parties, Cabinet, Whitehall) deny politics in the Arendtian sense through the promotion and delivery of one way of resolving the problem, and attacks on those who want to consider alternative forms of education and schooling. This puts barriers in the way of relational encounters, not least through using labour and work as the means by which to render humans as objects of reform. In the Academies Programme, this is visible in the insistence of the shift from experimentation to radical systemic reform in the face of evidence to the contrary or at least slow down (Gunter 2011). In relation to our two examples, we can identify how the idea of a public system of schools maintained by a LA is rapidly becoming unthinkable, and if it is thought about it is rendered unspeakable. Indeed, we have evidence that the Department will not engage with schools unless they are Academies. The displacement of professionals and locally elected representatives (but recognising the co-option of some members of these groups) by business and faith elites is based on a rejection of a 'system' with derogatory claims about bureaucracy and provider capture. The potential and necessity of democratic renewal is widely recognised (see Marquand 2004), but this requires a pluralism of ideas and positions that is not currently tolerated. The language and beliefs underpinning the justifications for Academies is about delivery rather than the capacity for spontaneity located in natality and pluralism:

> What, then, *is* 'action'? … Arendt's account of action in politics contains very considerable complexities. In *The Human Condition*, however, she is chiefly concerned with action as a basic human capacity, and at this level it is not too difficult to say what it is. It is a very broad category of human activity that covers interactions with other people that are not matters of routine behaviour but require personal initiative. However intelligible they may be in retrospect, actions are unpredictable before the event. Thus, jumping into a river to rescue someone is action, going to work is usually not. (Canovan 1992, 131)

While any radical change in school provision requires labour and work, the absence of action in regard to the Academies Programme renders it as routine. Our examples illuminate a drive for security through reliance on established notions of knowledge production within elite groups: how business people have know-how about teaching, learning and welfare, and how faith organisations know-how to discipline potential.

What the logic of our examples and argument are leading to is an assessment of how our polity is in danger:

> the world is constituted by our common and shared experiences of it; we can be in the world to the degree to which we implicitly trust that the orientations we follow are more or less also followed by others. This commonness of the world is the background against which the plurality of perspectives that constitute the political can emerge. Politics requires a background of commonality and the recognition of the plurality and perspectivality of the judgement of those who share this background commonality. It is over and against such a background that political action can unfold. Politicial action, action in concert, presupposes civic and political equality as well as the expression of the new and the unprecedented, the expression of that moment that distinguishes the doer from all others. Such an experience of the world signifies that individuals share in common a 'public realm,' a space of appearances in the world, constituted by the interplay of commonality and perspectivality, equality and distinction. (Benhabib 2000, 55–56)

We are losing the potential for a 'commonness of the world' because the people who are leading and profiting from academisation seem to experience the exercise of power differently from those who are labouring and working for academies. The Academies Programme is based on a totalising ideology of common sense beliefs held by elite groups and overtly converted individuals. The more that phrases like 'new freedoms' are stated the more unity around this as a reality is generated. Penetrating this is really difficult. While the self-interested and damaging conduct of some elite interests has been exposed (Beckett 2007) and there have been localised protests against academy conversion (Gunter 2011), it seems that political debate has been replaced by censure. As one of us has shown, the conditions for totalitarianism are always with us, and following Arendt's (2009) analysis, the process of crystallisations is evident in the modernisation of education (Gunter 2014).

This is not inevitable, and what Arendt's thinking does is to help researchers think about the purposes of their projects, and to challenge ways of thinking and accepted methodologies. In this sense, as researchers, we need to critically engage with our intellectual tools and how these are deployed in the field and at our desks. For example, Kohn (2005) synthesises Arendt's position as follows: 'hence action, as Arendt came to understand it, is largely missing from the tradition of political and philosophical thought established and handed down by these thinkers' (ix), and so social science may not be able to help the field to grasp the limitations of a politics of activity based on labour and work. So as researchers who overtly locate within the social sciences as critical policy scholars, we need to critique intellectual work and how the elite knowledge we use interplays with demands for democratisation within knowledge production (Apple 2013). What our thinking with and about academy conversion does is to expose the depoliticisation of the relationship between ideas, evidence and action, and how as 'critical secretaries' we can illuminate how the Academies Programme is an example of 'nonreformist reforms' (Apple 2013, 41–42). In doing this, we risk the wrath of our field, particularly since we are often exposing the role of researchers and professionals in making those reforms look to be reformist (Gunter 2012). The very adoption of the phrase 'Academies Programme' accepts a rationality that is not there, the use of 'convertor' for an academy suggests a benign change that disconnects from a wider conversion process outlined in this paper. At a time when research is meant to deliver evidence to inform policy and practice, we are engaging with a thinking process, and as such we will not deliver a set of recommendations for action. As Strong (2012) argues 'thinking is always result-less' (339), but it can enable us to focus on what is distinctive about a situation, and following Arendt, there is a need to make judgements about what is new. While academies are not new in the sense that different versions of the independent school have been introduced at different times over the past thirty years, what seems to be emerging as distinctive about the current version is the shift from entryism of a 'new' type of school towards the normalisation of the private provision of education for all.

## Summary

Claims and counter claims fill the literatures about academies and their place within wider reforms. Comprehensive schools are variously damned with Adonis (2012) claiming that they are 'a cancer at the heart of English society' (xii) while academies as the 'all-ability independent state school, with dynamic independent sponsors taking charge of their management ...' (xii) are lauded as the cure. However, this misrepresentation of the comprehensive school is evident in wider discourses (Benn 2011), and the centralisation process involved in the rapid expansion of academies post-2010 has been identified (Bangs, MacBeath, and Galton 2011). Research and commentary suggests that a process of privatisation is underway (Mortimore 2013), whereby Ravitch's (2010) u-turn as a neoliberal reformer is recognition that enthusiastic policy deliverers can recover from conversion. Such activity suggests that the politics of the Academies Programme has vitality and energy, and we would agree that the debate implies that promoters of academies are subject to critical review, and alternatives get an airing. However, the examples we have used are just two out of many where the politics of conversion is taking place without due recognition of the evidence base and discourses. Academies are being forced onto communities without local ballots (as happened with Grant Maintained Status from 1988), and without scrutiny of the claims made by those who have taken over public assets and the education process.

Arendtian analysis has generated new insights about academy conversion through revealing the denial of a robust political process, particularly through exposing flimsy claims to be doing something new. The dominance and revitalisation of elite interests in the provision of public education is based on a narrative of educational purposes that is seductive – we must do something about urban education – and, singular – what we must do is to produce a workforce capable of complying with our profit and missionary motives. Pluralism and natality generate imaginings of spontaneity, so integral to learning and creativity, but sadly missing from the politics of this reform. Our capacity as researchers to see through this is related to the intellectual tools we access and deploy in our conceptual and analytical actions. Underpinning our analysis are claims that we must be critical of the demands for researchers to labour and work, where knowledge production needs to be based on action as a form of scholarly activism.

## Acknowledgements

We would like to thank the British Academy and the ESRC for funding the projects that this paper has drawn on. We would like to thank Stephen Rayner for his detailed and helpful advice.

## References

Adonis, A. 2012. *Education, Education, Education. Reforming England's Schools.* London: Biteback Publishing.

Apple, M. W. 1993. *Official Knowledge.* New York: Routledge.

Apple, M. W. 2013. *Can Education Change Society?* New York: Routledge.

Arendt, H. 1958. *The Human Condition.* 2nd ed. Chicago: The University of Chicago Press.

Arendt, H. 2005. *The Promise of Politics.* New York: Schocken Books.

Arendt, H. 2009. *The Origins of Totalitarianism.* (1958, 2nd ed.). Garsington: Benediction Books.

Astle, J., and C. Ryan, eds. 2008. *Academies and the Future of State Education.* London: CentreForum.

Bangs, J., J. MacBeath, and M. Galton. 2011. *Reinventing Schools, Reforming Teaching.* London: Routledge.

Barker, B. 2010. *The Pendulum Swings.* Stoke-on-Trent: Trentham Books.

Beckett, F. 2007. *The Great City Academy Fraud.* London: Continuum.

Benhabib, S. 2000. *The Reluctant Modernism of Hannah Arendt.* Lanham, MD: Rowman and Littlefield Publishers.

Benn, M. 2011. *School Wars. The Battle for Britain's Education.* London: Verso.

Blunkett, D. 2000. *Blunkett Announces Locations for First Three Academies*, September 15 2000. London: DCSF. Accessed October 2 2009. www.dcsf.gov.uk/pns/DisplayPN.cgi?pn_id=2000_0396.

Canovan, M. 1992. *Hannah Arendt, A Reinterpretation of her Political Thought.* Cambridge: Cambridge University Press.

Courtney, S. 2013. "A Reflection on the Construction of a Typology of School Types." A paper presented to the joint University of Oslo and University of Education education policy seminar, University of Manchester, Manchester, September/October 2013.

Daniels, D. 2011. "From Reality to Vision: The 'Birth' of the Petchey Academy." In *The State and Education Policy: The Academies Programme*, edited by H. M. Gunter, 92–104. London: Continuum.

DCSF. 2009. *What are Academies?* Accessed October 28. www.standards.dfes.gov.uk/academies/what-are-academies/?version=1.

DfE. 2010. *The Case for School Freedom: National and International Evidence. (Gove, Mythbuster 2).* Accessed July 2. www.education.gov.uk/freeschools

DfE. 2013. *Schools White Paper.* Accessed December 9. http://www.education.gov.uk/schools/toolsandinitiatives/schoolswhitepaper.

Elliott, J. 2011. "The Birth of Norwich's First School Academy: A Case Study." In *The State and Education Policy: The Academies Programme*, edited by H. M. Gunter, 52–65. London: Continuum.

Gilbert, C. C. Husbands, B. Wigdortz, and B. Francis. 2013. *Unleashing Greatness. Getting the Best from an Academised System. The Report of the Academies Commission.* London: RSA and Pearson.

Gove, M. 2012. *Michael Gove Speech on Academies*. Accessed October 7 2013. https://www.gov.uk/government/speeches/michael-gove-speech-on-academies.

Gunter, H. M. 2005. *Leading Teachers*. London: Continuum.

Gunter, H. M., ed. 2011. *The State and Education Policy: The Academies Programme*. London: Continuum.

Gunter, H. M. 2012. *Leadership and the Reform of Education*. Bristol: Policy Press.

Gunter, H. M. 2014. *Educational Leadership and Hannah Arendt*. London: Routledge.

Hatcher, R. 2011. "Local Government Against Local Democracy: A Case Study of a Bid for Building Schools for the Future Funding for an Academy." In *The State and Education Policy: The Academies Programme*, edited by H. M. Gunter, 39–51. London: Continuum.

HM Government. 2010. *The Coalition: Our Programme for Government*. London: Cabinet Office. Accessed September 16 2013. https://www.gov.uk/government/uploads/system/uploads/attachment_data/file/78977/coalition_programme_for_government.pdf.

House of Commons. 2009. *Academies, Oral Evidence. 1st July 2009*. London: The Stationary Office.

Kohn, J. 2005. "Introduction." In *The Promise of Politics*, edited by H. Arendt, vii–xxxiii. New York: Schocken Books.

Leo, E., D. Galloway, and P. Hearne. 2010. *Academies and Educational Reform*. Bristol: Multilingual Matters.

Levinson, N. 2001. "The Paradox of Natality: Teaching in the Midst of Belatedness." In *Hannah Arendt and Education*, edited by M. Gordon, 11–36. Boulder, CO: Westview Press.

Marquand, D. 2004. *Decline of the Public*. Cambridge: Polity Press.

McGinity, R., and H. M. Gunter. 2012. "Living Improvement 2: A Case Study of a Secondary School in England." *Improving Schools* 15 (3): 228–244.

McGinity, R., and H. M. Gunter. Forthcoming. "New Practices and Old Hierarchies: Academy Conversion in a Successful English Secondary School." In *Understanding the field of educational leadership*, edited by P. Thomson. London: Routledge.

Mortimore, P. 2013. *Education Under Seige*. Bristol: Policy Press.

NAO (National Audit Office). 2007. *The Academies Programme*. London: The Stationary Office.

New Labour. 1997. *New Labour: Because Britain Deserves Better*. Accessed September 16 2013. http://www.labour-party.org.uk/manifestos/1997/1997-labour-manifesto.shtml

New Labour. 2001. *Ambitions for Britain*. Accessed September 16 2013. http://www.labour-party.org.uk/manifestos/2001/2001-labour-manifesto.shtml

Newman, J., and J. Clarke. 2009. *Publics, Politics and Power*. London: Sage.

Northampton Academy. n.d. *Tony Blair visits Northampton Academy*. Accessed May 27 2009. www.northampton-academy.org/news/tony-blair-visits-northampton-academy.

PwC (PricewaterhouseCoopers). 2008. *Academies Evaluation: Fifth Annual Report*. London: DCSF.

Ravitch, D. 2010. *The Death and Life of the Great American School System*. New York: Basic Books.

Scott, J. C. 1998. *Seeing Like a State*. New Haven, CT: Yale University Press.

SSAT. 2007. *City Technology Colleges: Conception and Legacy*. London: SSAT.

Stoker, G. 2006. *Why Politics Matter*. Basingstoke: Palgrave MacMillan.

Strong, T. B. 2012. *Politics Without Vision*. Chicago, IL: The University of Chicago Press.

Woods, P., G. Woods, and H. M. Gunter. 2007. "Academy Schools and Entrepreneurialism in Education." *Journal of Education Policy* 22 (2): 263–285.

Wrigley, T., and A. Kalambouka. 2013. *Academies and Achievement: Setting the Record Straight*. Accessed December 19. www.changingschools.org.uk.

# From city technology colleges to free schools: sponsoring new schools in England

Geoffrey Walford

*Department of Education, University of Oxford, Oxford, UK*

In England, Free Schools were announced as a dramatic way in which government policy has changed such that it is now possible for groups of parents, organisations or charities to start their own schools. They are seen as an attempt to stimulate to 'supply side' of the quasi-market of schools, but they are not the first such initiatives. In the long period of Conservative Government from 1979 to 1987, there were two specific attempts to encourage new schools through City Technology Colleges and sponsored grant-maintained schools. Both of these initiatives stalled at just 15 schools, but it is argued that their significance was far greater than their numerical strength would indicate and that they can be seen as for-runners of the Academies and Free Schools. All of these schools can be seen as examples of increased privatisation and selection, and they thus exhibit their own embedded forms of social (in)justice.

## Introduction

The last three decades have seen a process of almost continuous change in the organisation of secondary education in England. Successive Conservative, Labour and now coalition governments have reorganised the government-funded secondary sector such that there has been growing specialisation, selection and privatisation, with schools gradually being removed from the direct control of local authorities and new schools being established outside their control. The latest of these moves is the introduction of Free Schools, which are run by charitable trusts and sponsored by groups of parents, teachers or others, or by universities, private schools, religious organisations or companies. They are often seen as a dramatically new way of establishing new schools and encouraging the supply side of the quasi-market in schooling. But the Free Schools have several antecedents, which all relate to increasing privatisation and new forms of selection. This paper considers the rise of Free Schools in the longer historical context and considers the implications of these new schools in terms of social (in)justice.

## The development of state education in England

In England, the state became involved in the provision of education at a later stage than in most other developed countries. Before the nineteenth century, the education of children was considered to be the private affair of parents. The type of schooling that children received depended to a great extent on the social class of their parents, with children from the upper and middle classes attending a variety of private schools differentiated according to cost. There is some debate about the nature and extent of schooling for children of the working class. While most historians state that working-class children received little or no formal schooling, others (such as West 1994) argue that there is considerable evidence that a variety of charity schools linked to the churches or Dame schools provided schooling of a reasonable standard for the majority of children. Whatever is the case, as urbanisation and industrialisation increased throughout the eighteenth century, the sometimes contradictory drives of philanthropy, religious conviction and the practical need for a better trained and disciplined workforce led to the gradual expansion of a network of schools for the poor. In the early nineteenth century, there were various unsuccessful attempts to establish a national system of schools for working-class children, but it was not until 1833 that the government made its first donation to the two main religious providers of the day to help with the 'establishment of schoolhouses'. Regular government grants soon followed, and the Newcastle Commission of 1861 found that some 95% of children of the 'poorer classes' attended school, even if only for four to six years. The government started to build and maintain its own schools in 1870, and elementary education was made compulsory for all children in 1880.

It is important to recognise that the government only became involved in the provision of schooling because the charitable providers were unable or unwilling to provide for the children in the rapidly expanding cities (Ball 2012). In general, this reluctance of governments to fund schooling has not significantly changed over the centuries. The responsibility for provision was, and still is, shared by a multitude of providers – predominantly the Christian churches. The key 1944 Education Act for England and Wales built upon this existing understanding. To make it possible to provide secondary schooling for all children, it was seen as necessary to include as many as possible of the pre-existing secondary schools that were owned by the Church of England or the Roman Catholic Church within the state-maintained sector. While many religious schools remained as full private schools, the majority entered into arrangements with the state in one of three categories – voluntary controlled, voluntary aided or special agreement. The main distinction between the three was the degree of control that the Board of Governors maintained over the school and the size of the financial contribution expected from the Churches in return for this remaining control. This led to a key difference between England and many other developed countries – while these schools retained their religious denominational character, they became an integral part of the state-maintained local authority system and received the bulk of their running costs from the state. The 1944 Education Act also gave the churches the opportunity to build new primary and secondary schools and this was taken up vigorously by the churches (O'Keeffe 1986).

Although it was not stated in the 1944 Education Act, initially most local education authorities established selective systems of secondary schooling. While it was generally accepted that all children within the local area should be offered places in the same local primary schools differentiated by faith if desired (still giving those who wished the opportunity to attend private schools), by secondary schooling at 11 it was thought necessary to have a selective system based on performance on an 11 plus examination. Children were selected to attend grammar schools and, sometimes, technical schools if they did well on this examination. For those who 'passed' the examination and went to grammar schools, the expectation was that they would stay until 18 and might then go on to higher education. If they 'failed', they went to secondary modern schools where they usually left at 16. Thus places where made available for children with perceived high academic ability to attend grammar schools theoretically no matter how poor they were. The ideas of social justice at the time demanded that a 'ladder of opportunity' was offered to academically able and 'deserving' children from poor families. By the 1960s, ideas about selection had changed and this selective system was gradually replaced by a comprehensive one in most local education authorities.

Throughout the first four decades following the 1944 Act, new schools were established by the local education authorities and by religious providers in association with the local education authorities. Over the years, new voluntary controlled and aided schools were agreed with the local education authorities if there was deemed to be a demand for such schools. Most of these voluntary schools were provided by the Church of England and the Roman Catholic Church, but there were also some Jewish and Methodist schools and a very few non-religious schools that moved from the private sector. Technically, it was always possible for local education authorities to support various other religiously based schools through voluntary status. Although the 1944 Education Act was designed to protect the interests of the various Christian denominations, the legislation was such that other religious groups could also benefit. Support for some Jewish schools has been longstanding.

Many commentators incorrectly see the 1988 Education Reform Act as the crucial legislation that introduced new ways of establishing schools. It is certainly correct that this Act significantly restructured state-maintained schooling by creating more devolved management structures for schools, giving them greater autonomy, allowing families the right to express a preference for any state-maintained school they wish to use and funding schools largely according to the number of students each attracts. Together, such changes made the state-maintained schooling system more like that of the private sector. A 'quasi-market' was encouraged, where a greater emphasis was given to market forces and private decision-making (Le Grand and Bartlett 1993). Such developments have been common within the educational systems of industrialised countries around the world (Walford 1996; Whitty, Power, and Halpin 1998). However, in common with the schemes introduced in other countries, the 1988 Education Reform Act provided no new ways by which interested charitable or religious bodies could establish new state-maintained schools.

That this is true is not immediately obvious, for the 1988 Act included legislation on grant-maintained schools and City Technology Colleges. Both of these would appear to be supply-side developments, but the reality is different. While the concept of grant-maintained schools was certainly new, the reality was that existing local education authority schools were simply removed from the control of their local educational authorities and became funded by central government (eventually through the Funding Agency for Schools) instead. Much research has shown that grant-maintained schools generally offered little that was distinctive and rarely went beyond cosmetic changes such as smarter uniforms for students (Fitz, Halpin, and Power 1993; Halpin, Power, and Fitz 1997; Power, Halpin, and Fitz 1994). Local management of schools within the local authority sector meant that the grant-maintained schools differed only slightly from local authority schools in their degree of autonomy and hardly at all in the day-to-day experiences of staff or students.

On the other hand, the City Technology Colleges were certainly an attempt to increase the supply side of schooling. They were designed to be a significant new way of sponsoring and funding schools. But, as will be discussed further below, the 1988 Act's legislation on City Technology Colleges was merely making minor adjustments to a programme that was already under way – and which was already under pressure and liable to fail. The City Technology College programme had been launched in 1986, and the first CTC was announced in February 1987. So, while the 1988 Act is often seen as being the centrepiece of the Conservative government's quasi-market for schools, it actually included no new methods whereby potential sponsors could start new schools.

## City technology colleges

The initial public announcement of the City Technology Colleges was made during a speech by Kenneth Baker (then a new Secretary of State for Education) on 7 October 1986, at the Conservative Party Annual Conference. He outlined how a pilot network of twenty City Technology Colleges was to be created, which would be jointly funded by central government and industrial sponsors. The initiative was explicitly presented as one of a number of new measures that were intended to offer 'new hope and opportunity to selected young people and parents'. As the name suggests, City Technology Colleges were to provide a curriculum rich in science and technology, but they were also designed for a specific group of 11–18 year olds from the 'inner city'. One major feature was that they were to be private schools (officially designated as independent schools), run by independent charitable trusts, with the sponsors having a major influence on the way in which the colleges were managed. These sponsors were also intended to provide substantial financial and material support. While central government would provide recurrent funding on a scale similar to that of local authority schools, additional funding was expected to be provided by the private sponsors.

A brochure published by the Department of Education and Science (DES 1986) was sent to about 2000 leading industrial and commercial organisations asking them to support the venture. As has been discussed elsewhere (e.g. Walford and Miller 1991; Whitty, Edwards, and Gewirtz 1993), City Technology Colleges were firmly linked to the idea of widening and improving educational provision in urban areas, particularly the disadvantaged inner cities, where the government believed the local authority system was often failing children. While not explicit in the booklet, this was a concealed attack on the Labour councils which controlled practically all of the inner-city local education authorities.

The reaction to the announcement of CTCs was not as the government would have wished. Apart from the expected negative reactions from the teacher unions, the local education authorities and the Labour opposition, there were very few industrialists who showed their 'wish to help extend the range of choice for families in urban areas' (DES 1986, 3), and many who were openly hostile to the idea. It took until February 1987 for the first site and sponsor to be announced and a little later, just before a General Election, two more sponsorships were made public. All of these sponsors were regular supporters of the Conservative Party, but even they were unprepared to donate anything like the proportion of the funds that had been originally envisioned. Where the intention was that practically all of the capital expenditure would be provided by sponsors, they refused to give more than about 20%, leaving the government with a large, and unexpected, bill.

This reluctance to fund the CTCs accounts for their mention in the 1988 Education Reform Act. As the CTCs are officially independent schools, they required no new legislation; the government could simply use its existing powers to give funding to private schools as it wished. However, the ease with which funding could be granted had both positive and negative features, for it meant that another government could equally quickly cease to fund the CTCs if it wished. Even after the 1987 re-election of a Conservative government, fears of what a future Labour government might do led to clauses in the 1988 Act that began to protect the investment of sponsors. In practice, even with this safeguard, the scheme rapidly stalled. As is well known, the considerable difficulties in attracting sufficient sponsorship and in finding appropriate sites for the CTCs continued (Walford and Miller 1991; Whitty, Edwards, and Gewirtz 1993). The programme stalled at 15 CTCs with about only 20% of capital funding having been provided by sponsors and the bulk of the capital expenditure and practically all of the current expenditure being provided direct by central government.

At first sight, the CTCs appear to be a top-down initiative that went wrong. There appears to have been little consultation with potential sponsors from industry before the announcement, and their support was (incorrectly) assumed. The plan led to a great deal of controversy with local authorities and an unexpectedly large bill for central government. In practice, of course, although the degree of consultation was certainly inadequate, the CTC idea did not just appear from nowhere. Whitty, Edwards, and Gewirtz (1993) trace what they call the 'ideological ground-clearing' for the attack on local education authorities and the promotion of the market back to the foundation of the Institute of Economic Affairs in 1957, but it was not until the mid-1970s that pressure began to build for a greater role for market forces in schooling provision. The last two of the infamous *Back Papers on Education*, for example, included papers that called for educational vouchers (Boyson 1975) and greater choice and diversity within the schooling system (Sexton 1977).

More direct influences on the CTC initiative came from a variety of sources. One source was Stuart Sexton who had been political advisor to the two preceding Secretaries of State for Education – Keith Joseph and Mark Carlisle. For Sexton (1987, 1992), the technological aspect was of minor importance compared to his desire for per-capita funding of new schools outside the LEA system. But the technological emphasis was strong amongst industrialists who attended a Centre for Policy Studies conference organised by Cyril Taylor in January 1986 who called for the creation of 100 technical secondary schools to be funded by central government on a direct grant basis. Interestingly, again, these were to be initially focused on the 'deprived inner-city areas' and were to act as 'beacons' for other secondary schools (Taylor 1986, 20). Taylor, a businessman running an educational company and an ex-Greater London Council Councillor, went on to become the Chief Executive of the Technology Colleges Trust and its later reincarnations, which helped establish specialist schools. The challenge to the LEA system echoed Margaret Thatcher's views and also those of Brian Griffiths who was the head of the Prime Minister's Policy Unit at that time and had considerable influence. He was a firm advocate of education being opened to the rules of supply and demand and of business–school partnerships (Griffiths 1990). In the end, it seems that it was Kenneth Baker himself who contributed the idea of sponsorship of schools by business and industry. He saw sponsorship as a way to display a unique commitment and to create a 'direct relation between local employers and their schools' (Whitty, Edwards, and Gewirtz 1993, 21).

## Sponsored grant-maintained schools

It was not until the 1993 Education Act that any further changes were made to increase the supply side of the quasi-market. As a result of that Act, it became possible for groups of parents, and charitable, religious or independent sponsors to apply to the Secretary of State for Education in England or the Secretary of State for Wales to establish their own grant-maintained schools. According to the Government White Paper that preceded the Act, the explicit intentions behind such developments were to widen choice and diversity of schools and to allow new grant-maintained schools to be created 'in response to parental demand and on the basis of local proposals' (DFE 1992, 26). If the Secretary of State approved individual proposals, the way was opened for England and Wales to have state-funded schools that aimed to foster, for example, Muslim, Buddhist or evangelical Christian beliefs, or that wished to promote particular educational philosophies. Groups of sponsors could propose either an entirely new school or that an existing faith-based or other private school for which they were responsible should be re-established as a grant-maintained school. It is important that an account of these schools be given here as they are omitted in many accounts of the development of Free Schools (e.g. Chapman and Salokangas 2012; Chitty 2013; Ball 2012; Hatcher 2011). While not denying the influence and links to other initiatives such as Charter schools in the USA and Free Schools in Sweden, these sponsored grant-maintained schools must be seen as direct forbearers of the Free Schools from within the English system itself.

These sponsored grant-maintained schools differed from existing grant-maintained schools in that sponsors had to pay for at least 15% of costs relating to the provision of school buildings and some other capital expenditure. In return for this financial contribution, through the school's Trust Deed and Instrument of Governance, the sponsors could ensure that the school retained the purpose for which it was established. The composition of the governing body allowed the sponsors to ensure that the religious or other objectives of the school were maintained and that the religious beliefs and practices of teaching staff were taken into consideration in appointments.

Before this 1993 Act, while it was technically possible for local authorities to support new religiously based schools through voluntary-aided status, none were controlled by any other than mainstream Christian or Jewish religious groups. But the religious and ethnic composition of England had changed markedly since 1944 and several existing Muslim and evangelical Christian private schools had applied to their local authorities to become voluntary aided. All such applications had been rejected, which was a considerable challenge to various views of social justice as many Muslims have particular minority ethnic origins. The 1993 Act removed any barriers to the support of faith-based schools erected by local authorities and passed the decision directly to the Department for Education.

Within England, the process of application was long and difficult so that, even though there were many initial enquiries, by the time of the General Election in

May 1997, only 20 full proposals in England had been published. Only seven of these proposals had been successful – all but one were from existing private Roman Catholic secondary schools, the exception being an existing private Jewish primary school. At the time of the Election, only two applications had been rejected by the Secretary of State for Education, but two had been withdrawn and there were still ten applications outstanding. Some of these had been with the Secretary of State for over a year. At the same time, a further 15 or so promoters were in serious discussion with the Funding Agency for Schools.

While the CTCs initially had nobody from business or industry wishing to sponsor them, the sponsored grant-maintained schools had many potential sponsoring groups and existing private schools who were interested. Whereas the CTC can be seen as a 'top down' policy, the sponsored grant-maintained schools initially appear to be a 'bottom-up' initiative from the 'grass roots'. A long and very specific campaign by a diversity of pressure groups and individuals preceded the announcement of these sponsored grant-maintained schools (Walford 1995a, 1995b, 1995c), and many of those involved with CTCs were also highly influential in the campaign for sponsored grant-maintained schools. A full account of the campaign has been given elsewhere (Walford 1995a), but one of the major pressure groups involved was one representing several small private evangelical Christian schools. Several of those involved with the schools had developed links with active Christians within the House of Lords, House of Commons and in other prominent places. One who had a particularly close relationship with some of the schools was Baroness (Caroline) Cox, who was arguing for the right for religious minorities to establish their own schools funded by the state as early as 1981 (Marks and Cox 1981). Baroness Cox also played a crucial part in moving amendments to the 1993 Education Act, which removed an arbitrary restriction that would have made it impossible for sponsored grant-maintained schools to have been established in some local authorities.

When a Labour government was returned to power in 1997, it quickly produced a White Paper, *Excellence in Schools* (DFEE 1997), and the *School Standards and Framework Act* 1998 introduced a new organisational structure for schools. All grant-maintained schools were brought back into a revised local education authority system, and the Funding Agency for Schools was abolished. It also made it clear than no new proposals for sponsored grant-maintained schools would be considered, but that voluntary status would be possible. It finally accepted seven of the ten existing applications as voluntary-aided schools including two further Roman Catholic schools, one further Jewish schools and, much more significantly, two Muslim primary schools and one Seventh Day Adventist secondary school. It was thus Blair's government that made the decision to fund a greater range of schools for religious minorities. The Conservatives had brought forward the legislation, but, in the period before a General Election, they had not made any potentially controversial decisions. One of the schools rejected for sponsored grant-maintained status was the Maharishi school, which later became one the first 24 Free Schools to open in 2011.

The result is that in numerical terms the overall policy was not as successful as the original supporters of the 1993 legislation had hoped. Very few schools or sponsors managed to meet the demands made on them during the application process. Many fell by the wayside before their applications were passed to the Secretary of State for consideration, and only fourteen schools in England and one in Wales successfully became grant-maintained under these regulations. All but one of the sponsored grant-maintained schools involved the transfer of an existing private school into the state-maintained sector. The one entirely new school opened in September 1999, after grant-maintained status had been abolished.

## Academies

Given the difficulties that the Conservative government had experienced in trying to obtain sponsorship for CTCs, it is strange that Blair's Labour government should eventually resurrect the policy in the form of City Academies. In March 2000, David Blunkett, the Secretary of State, announced that 'City Academies' were to be created – officially independent schools, but maintained by the state. They were to have sponsors who would give £2million towards the capital costs and who would henceforth have a controlling interest in the school. This time they were not restricted to technology, but could also specialise in modern foreign languages, visual arts, performing arts or media arts, sport or 'any subject specified by order of the Secretary of State'. Their close similarity with the CTCs was emphasised by the fact that the legislation in the *Learning and Skills Act* 2000 simply amended the CTC legislation as it was in the *Education Act* 1996. As Chitty (2013, 122) argues, the City Academies were introduced by the highly unusual procedure of adding last-minute amendments to the *Education and Skills Bill 2000* after it had passed through the House of Lords. They were put forward as 'a radical approach' to 'breaking the cycle of underperformance and low expectations' and would replace 'seriously failing schools', which were to be found in the cities (Blunket 2010). All of this has strong echoes of the justification for CTCs.

Various difficulties with the policy led to further changes in the *Education Act* 2002 including the word 'City' being dropped such that these new schools became simply 'Academies' and could be established outside of cities as well. The first three Academies opened in 2002, nine more in 2003 and five more in 2004. In many ways, the initial story of the Academies echoed that of the CTCs, but from the start Blair's government was far more generous in its financial support and other assistance. Sponsors were able to donate 'in kind' to an extraordinary extent, and the average cost of the first 12 Academies was £23 million (Beckett 2007, 13). Faith groups saw this as an economical way of building their own schools, and the Blair government was active in trying to attract faith groups to become sponsors (Walford 2008). For a period, it seemed that the government's reluctance to fund schooling had been overturned and money poured into new buildings. But the fact that these schools were mainly funded through public–private partnerships, and thus would be paid for by future generations, is worthy of note.

Over the period of Labour government, the nature of Academies changed. At first, they were designed to replace existing failing schools, but, by 2004, the expectation had widened to include entirely new schools where there was a demand for new places. Such Academies were not called Free Schools at this point, but had many similarities for they allowed sponsors to start new schools. Later 'successful' private schools and universities were encouraged to become sponsors, and they were allowed to do so without any financial input.

At the end of Tony Blair's term in office, there were 83 Academies in operation, with many more due to open in future years, and a plan for 400 by 2010. Five of this total were re-named City Technology Colleges. It is worth noting that 27 of these could be defined as having a religious character. At 33%, this gives a similar percentage of faith schools to national figures for all schools. Nine of these were clearly Church of England, two clearly Roman Catholic, but there were 16 which are designated Christian, including one sponsored jointly by the Church of England and the Roman Catholic Church. Two of the Academies – The King's Academy and Trinity Academy – were sponsored by the Emmanuel Schools Foundation, which is the sponsoring body for Sir Peter Vardy's Emmanuel School (Green 2012). Critics have been particular concerned about these two Academies because of their strong evangelical Christian sponsorship, the teaching of creationism, high exclusion rates and homophobia (Beckett 2007, 68–85; Gillard 2007, 218). Another nine of these Academies were sponsored by the United Learning Trust, which is a Christian educational charity created specifically to sponsor academies and a subsidiary of the United Church Schools Trust, which was formerly the Church Schools Company founded in 1883 and currently controlling ten private schools England.

## Free schools

The Conservative–Liberal Coalition government that followed in 2010 moved the process of diversifying schools and making them 'independent' one stage further by introducing two new types of Academy. While the original Academies were based on the idea of closing poor schools and replacing them by dramatically redesigned and restructured ones, the *2010 Academies Act* allowed existing highly successful state-maintained schools to apply to become Academies as well. This allowed the schools to 'opt-out' of local authority control in a way reminiscent of the grant-maintained schools, but this time they were allowed to operate under regulations similar to private schools including not having to follow the National Curriculum and having their own salary scales and working condition for staff. They also did not have to find external sponsorship – indeed many schools clearly made the change in the expectation of extra funding from government. Further, while Labour restricted Academy status to secondary schools, the Coalition extended it to primary and special schools. The result is that there has been a dramatic increase in the number and diversity of Academies.

A further development to encourage the supply side of the market was Free Schools which are a new form of Academy which built on the ideas of sponsored grant-maintained schools and clarified that Academies could be entirely new schools. Here, groups of parents, teachers or other sponsors can apply to start their own state-maintained but officially 'independent' schools. These can either be completely new schools or existing private schools can apply to become state-maintained. They cannot charge fees once they become Free Schools.

The Coalition government mainly justified this development in terms of the perceived success of Free Schools (Friskolor) in Sweden. There more than 20% of all schools are free schools receiving per-capita funding from the state and usually run by parents and community groups in rural areas. Some of these schools are for-profit. There are also some chains of Friskolor including Kunskapsskolan, which has sponsored three new academies in England (Chapman and Salokangas 2012, 475). However, the idea is essentially the same as sponsored grant-maintained schools. The fact that only one new entirely school and 14 transferred private schools resulted from the Conservative government's 1993 legislation probably led to a reluctance to emphasise this similarity.

However, the early 2010s were different from the 1990s. Following 1993 the government and the then Department for Education and Employment showed reluctance to fund new schools. The application procedures were long and difficult, and many early applications were deterred on the first contact with the department. There was considerable concern about the funding of minority religious schools (Walford 2001). In contrast, the Conservative part of the Coalition in 2010 had a pledge to expand the Academies programme and to allow new types of school, and it funded the charitable New Schools Network, which was designed to help with Free School applications. Two factors outside their control also helped. First, the increase in the birth rate meant that many areas need new schools, and second, the downturn in the economy from 2008 onwards meant that many fee-paying private schools were under severe financial pressure. Not only did this mean that existing private schools threatened with closure might consider a transfer to the state sector, but also parents who might have been able to pay fees a few years earlier now considered starting their own private, but government-funded, schools.

In 2011, 24 Free Schools opened, followed by a further 55 in 2012. The range includes a Steiner school, a special school, several Jewish schools, a Muslim school, and many Christian schools of various denominations. There is also a growing emphasis on chains of schools with sponsors of several Academies now moving into Free Schools.

One recent example of a transfer to the state sector was King's School in North Tyneside (one of the Woodard group), which merged with a local state primary school to become an Academy. Existing debts of about £5 million were covered by the government (Mansell 2013).

## Social justice and selection

Selection of specific children for specific provision has been a central feature of all of these different types of school. It must be remembered that when the CTCs were introduced in 1986, most children were still allocated to nominally comprehensive schools through some form of catchment area system. In contrast, the CTCs were required to select children from a defined catchment area drawn such that about one in five or six of the relevant age population could be accommodated. They were explicitly not to be 'neighbourhood schools taking all comers', but the Head and governing body were to select applicants on the basis of:

> general aptitude, for example as reflected in their progress and achievements in primary school; on their readiness to take advantage of the type of education offered in CTCs; and on their parents' commitment to full-time education or training up to the age of 18, to the distinctive characteristics of the CTC curriculum, and to the ethos of the CTC. (DES 1986, 5)

Academic selectivity and a direct attack on comprehensive schooling, which might have acted as a vote-loser, was thus replaced by selection on a broad range of less easily measurable criteria which included parents' characteristics as well as those of their children. For a child to be accepted by a CTC, families needed to know about the Colleges and be able and prepared to negotiate the entrance procedures (which usually included a test and interview). Further, the children had to agree to work a longer school day, to attend for longer terms, and had to state that they intended to stay in education until 18. Thus, the CTCs were specifically selective schools, designed to benefit children from 'deserving' working-class families. Those families who could show themselves to be 'deserving' were far more likely to gain a place than others. Those children from families with little interest in education were ignored. This form of selection allowed the 'deserving' to be selected from the 'undeserving' and, just as importantly, helped to justify and 'normalise' the fact that some children *should* be selected to benefit from special facilities that are not available to those who are not selected (Walford 1997a). It is also worth noting that the children selected were not those who would necessarily go to university and professional occupations. The aim was to provide a technological education that would be suitable for those who would enter industry and technological jobs. There are implications here of providing schooling that is 'appropriate' for the particular class of children in these inner-city areas.

Selection also played a major part in sponsored grant-maintained schools. In this case, the results of the initiative have been to a large extent dependent upon the particular sponsors and schools that have applied. Yet, although the total was only 15 schools, many more schools and sponsors showed an initial interest. Some were encouraged and some not. Of the seven schools that were given sponsored grant-maintained status by the Conservative government, six of these could reasonably be called 'grammar schools' while the other one was a co-educational Jewish primary school. The six were all Roman Catholic schools and all had existing financial support from the state – either through Assisted Places (a specific Conservative scheme suspended by Labour) or through the local authority paying for RC 'grammar school' places to match the selective places available for non-RC children in the area.

Whether they are academically selective or not, religious schools introduce another layer of selection. The admissions process for sponsored grant-maintained schools gave preference to children from families with particular beliefs in the same way as existing Roman Catholic or Church of England voluntary schools. While the two Muslim primary schools would not see themselves as selective schools, they are allowed to ensure that their children come from homes where Islam is taken seriously and are thus able to select on this basis from the families that apply. In the same way, John Loughborough, the Seventh Day Adventist school in London that was given sponsored grant-maintained status, was able to select on the basis of adherence to Seventh Day Adventism. The school is a mainly black school, for Seventh Day Adventism has a largely black following in Britain. There are echoes here of places being provided for the 'deserving'. In all cases, the schools, parents and community have made substantial financial, work and time donations, and they have now been rewarded.

The original Academies are of interest because the aim was specifically to target schools perceived as failing and to replace them with new schools. Here, the target was the disadvantaged and the aim one that might be seen as directly in accord with social justice; however here again, it is these children who were seen as being able to benefit from the involvement of industry and commerce in their schooling. It was only later that it was seen as appropriate to involve universities and private schools who might be able to encourage enthusiasm for more academic pursuits. However, while the children selected for these new Academies may well have benefited from them (although the evidence is scant), the amount of money spent on these schools might well have been better spent on all of the schools in the area rather than being concentrated on just one school.

Selection continued to be a feature of the diversity of schools that developed during the Labour government with various specialist schools, Trust schools and the later forms of Academy. The selection is partly a matter of families having to apply for a place in these schools and thus having to have the knowledge and interest to negotiate the application process, and partly that the schools themselves have to show that they deserve to obtain sponsorship and extra funding. Specialist schools were also allowed to select a proportion of their intakes based on 'aptitude' in the particular specialism. Even after entry, selection continued to operate by schools rigidly enforcing rules, demanding high involvement with the schools and the common use of exclusions.

Selection has continued with the Coalition's Academies and, even more so, the Free Schools. With the private schools moving into the state-maintained system, parents have been able to pay for one or two years of private schooling (with all of the selectivity that that entails) and then been able to ensure that their child remains in the same school without payment of fees for the rest of their school careers. With the entirely new Free Schools, parents, teachers and others have been able to construct schools that have a particular appeal to certain types of families. For example, the West London Free School linked to Toby Young is described as a comprehensive school, but one that 'specialises in music, humanities and classical civilisation, with every student learning Latin up to age 14' (Hatcher 2011, 494). While this may be attractive to middle-class professions, it is unlikely to be attractive to the full range of families in West London. Religious Free Schools are also able to select a proportion of their intakes (usually 50%) on the basis of religion. For example, two schools in Handsworth, Birmingham, were sponsored by the Guru Nanak gurdwara and are able to select 50% on the basis of being Sikh. The other 50% are open to anyone, but are predominantly taken by Sikhs as well.

## Privatisation

Privatisation was one of the major policy priorities of successive governments since 1979, and its extension to education has taken many different forms (Walford 1997b). But its main feature has been that of supporting the private sector financially and ideologically while also encouraging private investment in the state-maintained sector to replace government funding, which is gradually withdrawn. Thus, the state-maintained sector has seen, for example, contracting out of services, increasingly inadequate funding and a growing need for schools to beg for support from industry, parents and the local community.

City Technology Colleges, sponsored grant-maintained schools, Academies and Free Schools, can all be seen as privatisation measures. One of the major aims of these initiatives was that sponsors would fund a substantial part of the initial capital costs and continue to make a contribution to recurrent expenditure. The fact that sponsors actually only contribute a small percentage of the initial costs and usually make small further additions does not change the nature of the policy. But the private nature of these schools has broader effects than just the directly financial. Their private school status allows the schools considerable flexibility in staffing, curriculum and management issues (Walford 1991). Teachers are not necessarily employed on standard national salaries, nor are unions necessarily recognised. Further, non-teacher-trained staff can be employed as teachers and as other employees with teaching and managerial responsibilities. Governing bodies are more mixed, and there is often industrial and commercial involvement with no link to the local authorities. Accountability is imprecise.

While building new schools with the support of sponsors can easily be seen as a special case of privatisation, bringing existing private schools into the state-maintained sector might be seen initially as the very opposite. In practice, however, both processes have elements of privatisation and may add to inequities associated with such processes. Here, privatisation occurs in the governance, management and provision of government-funded schooling.

The various attempts by groups of sponsors to start entirely new schools also illustrate the privatisation aspect of the policies. Sponsors of new schools have to have the energy and enthusiasm to establish the school and make it successful. It is also clear that that the larger the proportion of the capital costs that sponsors can provide, the more likely they are to be successful.

**Conclusion**

This paper has traced the development of Academies and Free Schools back to the early attempts to encourage the supply side of the quasi-market with City Technology Colleges and sponsored grant-maintained schools. Both of the early attempts must, in themselves, be seen as failures as only 15 of each were ever opened. However, their importance can be seen in their being precursors to local management of schools, delegated budgets, per-capita funding, decreased roles for local authorities, increased emphasis on selection for inequitable provision and greater specialisation between schools. The significance of both of these early initiatives far outweighs the limited number of schools and children that were involved, as they led to the Academies and Free Schools that are now a central feature of the English system. In particular, the acceptance of religious minority sponsored grant-maintained schools marked a turning point in the way schools are provided to support such groups. They also re-emphasised selection in schooling but in more complex ways than before. 'Aptitude' rather than ability was the cornerstone of this selection and those who were to be rewarded were those whose families were sufficiently knowledgeable and concerned about schooling to apply and become selected. This automatically leads to greater social injustice as parents compete (or decline to compete) for places.

Over the last decades, privatisation of schooling has occurred in a variety of different forms including private funding, provision, management and ownership of schools. One long-term concern is that we have seen that, with just a few exceptions, successive governments have usually shown reluctance to fund schooling and have tried to pass some of the responsibility to others. Currently, government is funding current expenditure for Academies and Free Schools on roughly the same basis as local authority schools. In the future, if government reluctance returns, we can expect the funding given to all schools to gradually decrease, and there to be an increased dependence on private funding of various sorts to make up for the deficits. Schools will thus become further differentiated and social injustice increase.

**Note**

This paper draws upon and develops several of my earlier papers (Walford 2000, 2001, 2008).

**References**

Ball, S. J. 2012. "The Reluctant State and the Beginning of the End of State Education." *Journal of Educational Administration and History* 44 (2): 89–103.
Beckett, F. 2007. *The Great City Academy Fraud*. London: Faber & Faber.
Blunket, D. 2010. "Speech to Social Market Foundation." March 15.
Boyson, R. 1975. "The Developing Case for the Educational Voucher." In *The Fight for Education. Black Paper 1975*, edited by C. B. Cox and R. Boyson. London: Dent.
Chapman, C., and M. Salokangas. 2012. "Independent State-funded Schools: Some Reflections on Recent Developments." *School Leadership and Management* 32 (5): 473–486.
Chitty, C. 2013. *New Labour and Secondary Education 1994–2010*. New York: Palgrave Macmillan.
DFE (Department for Education). 1992. *Choice and Diversity*. London: HMSO.
DFEE (Department for Education and Employment). 1997. *Excellence in Schools*. London: The Stationary Office (July).
DES (Department of Education and Science). 1986. *City Technology Colleges: A New Choice of School*. London: DES.
Fitz, J., D. Halpin, and S. Power. 1993. *Grant Maintained Schools. Education in the Market Place*. London: Kogan.
Gillard, D. 2007. "Never Mind the Evidence: Blair's Obsession with Faith Schools." *Forum* 49 (3): 213–228.
Green, E. 2012. "Analysing Religion and Education in Christian Academies." *British Journal of Sociology of Education* 33 (3): 391–407.
Griffiths, B. 1990. "The Conservative Quadrilateral." In *Christianity and Conservatism*, edited by M. Alison and D. L. Edwards. London: Hodder and Stoughton.
Halpin, D., S. Power, and J. Fitz. 1997. "Opting into the Past? Grant-maintained Schools and the Reinvention of Tradition." In *Choice and Diversity in Schooling*, edited by Ron Glatter, Philip A. Woods and Carl Bagley. London: Routledge.
Hatcher, R. 2011. "The Conservative-liberal Democrat Coalition government's 'Free Schools' in England." *Educational Review* 63 (4): 485–503.
Le Grand, J., and W. Bartlett, eds. 1993. *Quasi-markets and Social Policy*. London: Macmillan.
Mansell, W. 2013. "Private School's £5 M Debts Paid off as it becomes and Academy." *The Guardian* 12 August.
Marks, J., and C. Cox. 1981. "Education Allowances: Power to the People?" In *The Pied Pipers of Education*, edited by A. Flew, J. Marks, C. Cox, J. Honey, D. O'Keeffe, G. Dawson, and D. Anderson. London: Social Affairs Unit.
O'Keeffe, B. 1986. *Faith, Culture and the Dual System*. London: Falmer.
Power, S., D. Halpin, and J. Fitz. 1994. "Parents, Pupils and Grant-Maintained Schools." *British Educational Research Journal* 20 (2): 209–225.
Sexton, S. 1977. "Evolution by Choice." In *Black Paper 1977*, edited by C. B. Cox and R. Boyson. London: Temple Smith.
Sexton, S. 1987. *Our Schools – A Radical Policy*. Warlingham: Institute for Economic Affairs Education Unit.

Sexton, S. 1992. *Our Schools - Future Policy*. Warlingham: IPSET Education Unit, Chapman and Salokanges.

Taylor, C. 1986. *Employment Examined: The Right Approach to More Jobs*. London: Centre for Policy Studies.

Walford, G. 1991. "City Technology Colleges: A Private Magnetism." In *Private Schooling: Tradition, Change and Diversity*, edited by Geoffrey Walford. London: Paul Chapman.

Walford, G. 1995a. "The Christian Schools Campaign – A Successful Educational Pressure Group?" *British Educational Research Journal* 21 (4): 451–464.

Walford, G. 1995b. "The Northbourne Amendments: Is the House of Lords a Garbage Can?" *Journal of Education Policy* 10 (4): 413–425.

Walford, G. 1995c. *Educational Politics. Pressure Groups and Faith-based Schools*. Aldershot: Avebury.

Walford, G., ed. 1996. *School Choice and the Quasi-market*. Wallingford: Triangle Books.

Walford, G. 1997a. "Privatization and Selection." In *Affirming the Comprehensive*, edited by Richard Pring and Geoffrey Walford. London: Falmer.

Walford, G. 1997b. "Sponsored Grant-maintained Schools: Extending the Franchise?" *Oxford Review of Education* 23 (1): 31–44.

Walford, G. 2000. "From City Technology Colleges to Sponsored Grant-maintained Schools." *Oxford Review of Education* 26 (2): 145–158.

Walford, G. 2001. "Durkheim, Democracy and Diversity: Some Thoughts on Recent Changes in England and Wales." In *Emile Durkheim: Critical Assessments of Leading Sociologists*. Vol. VI, edited by W. S. F. Pickering, 543–559. London: Routledge.

Walford, G. 2008. "Faith-based Schools in England after Ten Years of Tony Blair." *Oxford Review of Education* 34 (6): 689–699.

Walford, G., and H. Miller. 1991. *City Technology College*. Buckingham: Open University Press.

West, E. G. 1994. *Education and the State. A Study in Political Economy*. 3rd ed. Indianapolis, IN: Liberty Fund.

Whitty, G., T. Edwards, and S. Gewirtz. 1993. *Specialisation and Choice in Urban Education. The City Technology College Experiment*. London: Routledge.

Whitty, G., S. Power, and D. Halpin. 1998. *Devolution and Choice in Education. The School, the State and the Market*. Buckingham: Open University Press.

# Academies in England and independent schools (*fristående skolor*) in Sweden: policy, privatisation, access and segregation

Anne West

*Education Research Group, Department of Social Policy, London School of Economics and Political Science, London, UK*

Academies (and free schools) in England and independent grant-aided schools, *fristående skolor* (or *friskolor*), in Sweden have been the subject of much academic debate, but there is a paucity of comparative research relating to policy development or outcomes. This paper adopts a comparative perspective, outlining the historical context, then comparing the policy goals and development of the two programmes from their inception. It is argued that the policy goals of the two programmes are underpinned by similar ideologies, but the policy outcomes have differed in terms of the extent and type of 'privatisation'. Two broad themes related to equality of opportunity are then explored: access to schools, and school composition and segregation. It is argued that the extent to which differential school access and segregation can be attributed to the introduction of independent schools in Sweden and academies in England, is far from clear; it would be wrong to assume that there is a single, simple explanation.

## Introduction

In countries as diverse as England, Sweden and the United States, school-based education is undergoing significant changes in terms of the delivery of education, with private providers increasingly taking over from public providers. In England, academies have been introduced; in Sweden, grant-aided independent schools (*fristående skolor*) colloquially known as *friskolor* have been introduced; and in the USA charter schools have been established (Lubienski 2013; Zimmer et al. 2009). These changes are significant not least because they represent the influence of a particular set of ideas about the provision of education. They are also important in terms of what they portend for the role of the state in the provision of school-based education.

This paper focuses on two countries, England and Sweden. In both cases the school-based education system has been transformed with an increased focus on parental choice of school, school autonomy and competition. Whilst England and Sweden differ in terms of their education systems (Green, Preston, and Janmaat 2006; West and Nikolai 2013), in both countries, from the 1980s neo-liberal ideas began to take hold and played a significant role in the development of education policy.

Neo-liberal ideas are associated with policy goals that include the commodification and privatisation of public assets (Harvey 2005) and specifically with regards to education, privatising education services and introducing competition, which it is argued will lead to 'better schools, and hence better education for all students, closing the achievement gap' (Hursh 2007, 498). In both England and Sweden there have been moves to introduce competition and choice into the school-based education system.

An important feature in both England and Sweden has been the 'privatisation' of educational assets. Whilst the notion of privatisation has been construed in many ways (see Lubienski 2013; Lundqvist 1988; Power and Taylor 2013), it is used here to refer to the transfer of school ownership and the delivery of education from public to private (i.e. not public) bodies (cf. Blomqvist 2004). In both countries, new schools have been developed, owned by private bodies, but publicly funded and subject to differing degrees of government regulation. Indeed, the introduction of one new type of school in England, the free school, was justified with explicit reference to Swedish 'free schools' (Department for Education 2010). Whilst the broad policy goals were not dissimilar, the policy implementation and outcomes for Sweden and England have differed, particularly with respect to the role of for-profit providers; there are both for-profit and non-profit providers in Sweden, but only non-profit providers in England (West and Bailey 2013). In both countries debates about the impact of these policy changes with respect to access and school segregation continue unabated.

This paper focuses specifically on the development of two types of privatised schools: academies (including free schools, a type of academy) in England and independent schools (*fristående skolor* or *friskolor*) in Sweden. The analysis presented is based, in the main, on published material, including policy documents, statistics and academic literature, supplemented by information provided by five expert interviewees from Swedish central and local government.

The paper seeks to answer the following research questions:

- What were the policy goals for academies in England and independent schools in Sweden? How has policy developed over time?
- To what extent is there equal access to academies and independent schools in England and Sweden? How does school composition vary and why?

Following a brief outline of the historical context in each country, the paper compares and contrasts the policy goals, the legislative frameworks and the development of academies in England and independent schools in Sweden. The paper then addresses two broad themes relating to equality of opportunity: school access on one hand and school composition and segregation on the other. The final section concludes.

## Historical context

In order to understand the development of education policy, it is important to consider the role of the state in the provision, regulation and financing of schools. Thus, in Sweden, from 1842 every parish was required to establish at least one elementary school, and in 1880, school attendance became compulsory between the ages of 7 and 13 (Fägerlind and Saha 1989). In England, the church was also historically a key player in the provision of education, with the state taking on an increasing role from the late nineteenth century (Gordon, Aldrich, and Dean 1991); however, it was not until 1918 that all fees were abolished in elementary schools and education from the ages of 5 to 14 became compulsory. During the first half of the twentieth century legislative and policy changes took place in both countries, with those in the 1940s being highly significant, particularly with respect to academic selection and the role of the church.

In Sweden, the education reforms in the 1940s–1970s were seen to be crucial to the construction of the welfare state (Lundahl 2005). In 1948, a proposal was made by the social democratic prime minister for a single compulsory nine year comprehensive school that would replace all schools catering for pupils between the ages of 7 and 16 (Fägerlind and Saha 1989). One of the key goals of the comprehensive reform was equality of opportunity between social classes and between rural and urban areas. The 1950 Education Act provided for a 10 year pilot programme involving the integration of elementary and lower secondary schools (Husén 1986). The evaluation revealed that pupils who had attended comprehensive schools in Stockholm had the same levels of achievement as those in grammar schools (having controlled for socio-economic background and prior ability). Following this, in 1962, the decision was taken to implement comprehensive education across the country. By 1972 comprehensivisation was fully implemented (Fägerlind and Saha 1989; Husén 1986).

In England, the 1944 Education Act set up a universal system of free, compulsory education for children aged 5–15,[1] comprising primary and secondary schools. Some had a religious character and more autonomy, particularly with respect to admissions.[2] The Act also allowed for the implementation of a selective system of secondary education (grammar, technical and secondary modern schools),[3] with admission being based, in the main, on the results of an ability test taken at the age of 11. However, concerns about a disproportionate number of places being allocated to children from middle-class backgrounds led to a request by the Labour Government in 1965 for LEAs to submit plans for the introduction of comprehensive secondary education. By the early 1980s comprehensive education was almost universal, although some authorities retained grammar schools (Simon 1991). In England, ideas relating to equality of opportunity were important, although understandings varied: equal access to the more advanced stages of education for all children, regardless of their sex or social origin; equal access to appropriate secondary schools, according to the age, aptitude and ability; and access to an appropriate education within a common comprehensive school (see Silver 1973).

## Policy goals, policy development since the 1980s

During the late 1980s and early 1990s significant changes took place in school-based education in both Sweden and England, with governments on the right of the political spectrum introducing a range of policies designed to increase choice and competition. The changes took place at different times and in different ways. They have been more gradual in Sweden than in England, but arguably the changes in the former represent a more significant change as for-profit schools have been introduced.

### *Sweden*

During the 1980s, the centrally regulated publicly-funded school system became a key issue for the Social Democrat Government. The 1985 Education Act

(1985:1100) was particularly significant, stressing as it did, the need for 'equivalent' education:[4]

> All children and young persons shall irrespective of gender, geographic residence and social and financial circumstances have equal access to education in the national school system for children and young persons. The education shall be of equal standard within each type of school, wherever in the country it is provided. (S. 2)

During this period, concerns were expressed by the public about the difficulty parents had sending their child to a school of their choice, and a raft of proposals for school reform were put forward. Decentralisation and a new funding system were introduced: funding was delegated to municipalities via an unhypothecated block grant for schools and education enabling them to make decisions as to how to use funds allocated by central government. With respect to choice, all schools were given an opportunity to develop special 'profiles' (including specific linguistic or religious orientations) and were required to meet individual preferences insofar as this was practically and economically feasible (Klitgaard 2009).

Education policy underwent a more significant change in the 1990s following the election of a Liberal-Conservative Government in 1991:

> Pressures for a shift in policy values and emphasis – from equality to choice – gained new momentum in the 1990s, triggered by ideological and social change. Parental choice was in tune with the individualism promoted in neoliberal policy and ideology ... (Ellingsaeter and Leira 2006, 269)

Between 1991 and 1994, the government championed neo-liberal policies, with the expressed aim of increasing the role of independent schools in the school system (Skolverket 2006). Proposition[5] 1991/92:95 *Choice and Independent Schools*, allowed independent fee-charging schools to receive a per pupil amount equivalent to 85% of the costs of a public school pupil, and to cover the remaining amount by charging parents an additional school fee.

In 1992, the Conservative Swedish School Minister (Ask 1992, 102, 104) stated: 'The work with developing and expanding freedom of choice carries on both in the government and out in the municipalities' and a 'school system – based on the free choice of students and parents – is far better than the pacifying school monopoly that we have had ...'. Thus, the Liberal-Conservative Government gave parents increased possibilities to choose between schools. The state monopoly was broken and choice and market-oriented reforms were implemented (Lundahl 2002).

Policy goals for the Swedish reforms have been summarised as freedom of choice, higher quality education and greater cost-effectiveness. First, by creating a wider range of schools (including those with a religious profile and those run by private for-profit companies) freedom of choice would be increased: this was seen as a goal in its own right and a means of achieving other aims. Second, by allowing different providers and schools with different specialisations (profiles) into the system, schools would compete with one another so improving the quality of the school system. A third goal was a more cost effective school system, via the more effective use of resources such as disseminating cost-effective working methods (Skolverket 2006).

The Social Democratic Government, elected in 1994 continued these policies, also believing that competition and choice would be beneficial. They reduced the state contribution to 75% but decided two years later that independent schools should be granted public funding on a per pupil basis at an amount equivalent to the cost per pupil in the public schools. However, parents could no longer be charged fees (Klitgaard 2009). The government also expressed the need for a 'consistent and equivalent school system and public control of this' (Skolverket 2006, 13).

Independent schools must be approved by the Swedish Schools Inspectorate and must not charge fees; once established they receive funding on a per capita basis (a form of quasi-voucher) from the home municipality of the pupils who attend (Eurypedia 2013). Until the implementation of the 2010 Education Act, there were important differences between independent schools and municipality schools (see Arreman and Holm 2011). However, since then independent schools have had to comply, as far as possible, with the same regulatory framework as municipality schools (Regeringskansliet Government Offices of Sweden 2009, 1), and are bound by various ordinances and curricula (Båvner et al. 2011).

*Numbers and ownership*

The number of independent schools has increased gradually over time as shown in Figures 1 and 2 (see also Appendix 1). At the beginning of the 1991/92 school year there were around 89 comprehensive independent schools (including Montessori, Waldorf, religion-oriented and international schools) (Miron 1993), and by 2012/13 790 (16%) (Skolverket 2013). At the upper secondary level in 1992/93, there were around 59 independent schools (Miron 1993), and by 2012/13 there were 485 (39%) (Skolverket 2013). The concentration of independent schools is greatest in the large urban conurbations, Stockholm, Malmö and Gothenburg.

The owners of independent schools are of different types as shown in Table 1.

A majority of independent schools are owned by a corporation/stock market company: 58% of comprehensive schools and 87% of upper secondary independent

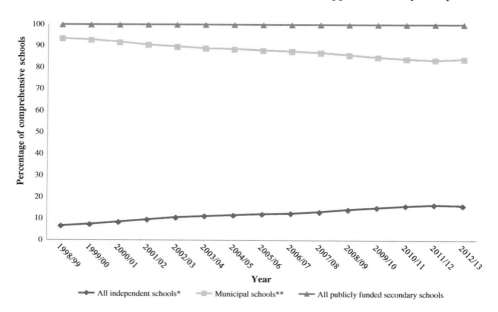

Figure 1.   Proportion of comprehensive schools in Sweden by type (1999–2013).
Source: Skolverket (2004, 2005, 2010, 2013).

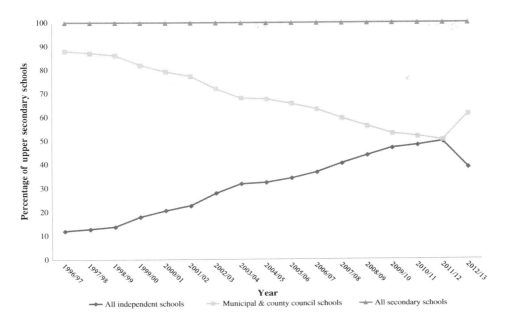

Figure 2.   Proportion of upper secondary schools in Sweden by type (1997–2013).
Source: Skolverket (2005, 2010, 2013).

Table 1.   Type of providers of independent comprehensive schools and upper secondary
schools in Sweden (percentage table).

| Providers | Comprehensive schools (N = 800) | Upper secondary schools (N = 494) |
|---|---|---|
| Corporation/Stock company | 58 | 87 |
| Economic partnership | 16 | 1 |
| Non-Profit association | 13 | 3 |
| Foundation | 12 | 8 |
| Individual | <1 | 0 |
| Religious community | <1 | 0 |
| Other (e.g. Official Corporation, General Partnership, Sole Proprietorship, Private Unregistered Firm and Single Proprietorship) | <1 | 1 |

Source: Skolinspektionen (2013).

schools.[6] Other types of owners include foundations (12% and 8%) and non-profit
associations (13% vs. 3%). All organisational forms can be for profit, except for the
'non-profit' association.


*England*

In England, major changes took place under successive Conservative administrations
between 1979 and 1997, with neo-liberal ideas influencing education policy.

Individualism came to the fore, with parental choice having a greater priority than previously, competition between schools being fostered and school autonomy incentivised. Quality, diversity, parental choice, greater school autonomy and greater accountability were key policy themes (Department for Education/Welsh Office 1992). Underpinning the reforms was the view that parents would choose the 'best' schools for their child, based on the information available – in particular, national test and examination results – and that the ensuing competition between schools would result in higher educational standards. These changes were underpinned by the 1980 Education Act and the 1988 Education Reform Act, which created a 'quasi-market' (Le Grand and Bartlett 1993): parents were able to make 'choices' (preferences) for schools; schools became funded predominantly on the basis of the number of pupils enrolled; pupils were to be admitted up to the limit of the school's physical capacity; and national test and public examination 'league tables' were published. Schools were thus incentivised to increase the number of pupils enrolled and maximise their 'league table' position. They could also 'opt out' of LEA control and become 'grant maintained', funded by central government, and taking control of admissions.

In addition, independent city technology colleges (CTCs) were established.[7] CTCs represented a new institutional form: they were private, non-profit bodies funded by central government not via LEAs. The original intention was for private sector sponsors to meet the capital costs with the revenue costs being met by the government via a contract (funding agreement), but few sponsors were willing to fund the full capital costs of the schools (Walford 2000; Whitty, Edwards, and Gewirtz 1993). Only 15 CTCs were established.

With the election of a Labour Government in 1997 continuity was maintained with respect to the main tenets of the education quasi-market.[8] According to the White Paper 'Higher Standards Better Schools For All':

> Our reforms must build on the freedoms that schools have increasingly received, but extend them radically. We must put parents in the driving seat for change in all-ability schools that retain the comprehensive principle of non-selection … And to underpin this change, the local authority must move from being a provider of education to being its local commissioner and the champion of parent choice. (DfES 2005, Foreword)

The Labour Government also established academies,[9] independent schools akin to CTCs being outside LEA control, bound by a funding agreement with the Secretary of State with responsibility for education, and set up by external sponsors. Academies unlike CTCs were (initially) designed as a school improvement policy tool (see also Gorard 2009; West and Bailey 2013). Thus, the institutional form introduced by the Conservative Government – the CTC – was resurrected and revised with a different function.[10] Academies were sponsored (e.g. by businesses or individuals); initially sponsors were expected to make a contribution of around 20% of the capital costs, but this was later changed to an endowment fund, with exemptions being made for certain types of sponsor (e.g. universities). Finally, in 2009 the requirement for sponsors to make financial contributions to new academies was removed (National Audit Office 2010).

Following the 2010 general election, the Conservative-Liberal Democrat Coalition Government extended the academies programme: in addition to sponsored academies, other forms of academy were introduced, including primary academies. The

2010 Academies Act allowed for state-maintained schools to convert to academy status. It also allowed for the introduction of 'free' schools – all-ability publicly-funded schools. A free school can be set up by a group that can provide evidence of parental demand, via for example a petition. Groups can include community or faith groups; parents; teachers; charities; businesses; universities; and private, fee-charging schools (Gov.uk 2013). The debates surrounding the introduction of free schools drew on the Swedish developments. Indeed, the White Paper 'The importance of teaching' (DfE 2010) made explicit reference to Swedish free schools, a clear example of policy borrowing.

The 2010 Academies Act also allowed for the introduction of university technical colleges and studio schools for 14- to 19-year-olds (the former backed by university and employer sponsors and the latter by local businesses and employers (see DfE 2013a)).

There are important differences between academies and other types of publicly-funded schools. All types of academies, including free schools are owned by non-profit trusts[11] and funded by a legal contract (funding agreement) with the Secretary of State for Education. They are also responsible for their own admissions. They are not required to adhere to the national curriculum (they must have a 'balanced and broadly based' curriculum), or regulations relating to teachers' pay. Under the Labour government they also had a specialism (e.g. technology, languages, arts and sports) and like all schools with a specialism could select a proportion of pupils on the basis of aptitude in the specialist subject area (see West and Bailey 2013).

*Numbers and ownership*

Figure 3 presents the number of secondary schools including different types of academies over time (see also Appendix 1, Table A3). In January 2003, there were only three academies; in 2010, prior to the legislation allowing schools to convert to academies 6% of secondary schools were academies; and by January 2013, 50% of secondary schools were academies. The massive increase is related to the introduction of converter academies, with the financial benefits associated with conversion being a significant factor in the decision to convert (Bassett et al. 2012).

There are proportionately fewer primary academies, which were introduced following the 2010 Academies Act; by 2013, there were 1006, 6% of all primary schools in England.

Free schools were also introduced following the 2010 Academies Act and since 2011, 174 have opened (primary, secondary and all-through schools (primary and secondary)) (DfE 2013d).

Turning to sponsored academies, these can be sponsored by different bodies: private individuals, private organisations, educational companies, successful schools, further education colleges, universities and local authorities (although a local authority[12] (LA) cannot be a lead sponsor) (see Curtis et al. 2008). However, the academies themselves cannot charge fees. Table 2 provides information on the organisations sponsoring more than three academies. The biggest are the Academies Enterprise Trust (AET), the Ormiston Academies Trust, United Learning (which has a Christian ethos), E-ACT, the Harris Federation, Oasis Community Learning (a Christian organisation) and Absolute Return for Kids (ARK). One Swedish chain, which owns (for-profit) independent schools in Sweden, *Kunskaps-skolan*, is a sponsor of three academies. In the case of 30 academies a diocesan

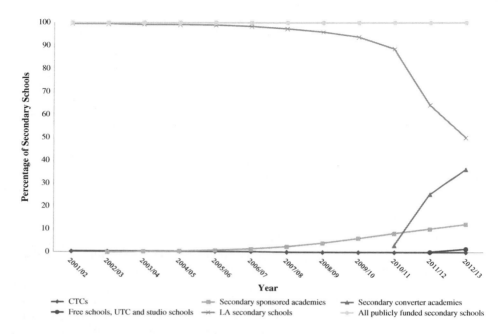

Figure 3.  Proportion of secondary schools in England by type January 2002–January 2013. Source: West and Bailey (2013) and DfE (2012b, 2013b).

Table 2.  Sponsors of more than three academies.

| Sponsors of >3 academies | Number of academies |
| --- | --- |
| AET | 29 |
| Ormiston Trust | 19 |
| United Learning | 18 |
| E-ACT | 18 |
| Harris | 12 |
| Oasis | 10 |
| ARK | 7 |
| Schools Partnership Trust | 6 |
| Cabot Learning Federation | 6 |
| Greenwood Dale Foundation Trust | 5 |
| Outwood Grange | 5 |
| University of Chester | 5 |
| ATT | 4 |
| David Ross Education Trust | 4 |

Source: DfE (2013c).

board is one of the sponsors; and 19 academies have an LA sponsor (along with, e.g. a further education college, university or a diocesan board).

Thus, in both England and Sweden, a raft of policy changes were implemented by governments of different political persuasions, from the late 1980s/early 1990s onwards. In both countries, the underpinning political ideology was that of neo-liberalism.

## Equality of opportunity: access, segregation and school composition

If schools compete with one another, it is not unreasonable to suppose that a hierarchy will result as individual schools will seek to enhance their position in the 'market'. Given the strong links between social background and educational attainment, schools are likely, given the opportunity, to seek to educate some pupils as opposed to others. If there are opportunities for selecting pupils via the admissions process, schools may seek to select those who are easier to teach and likely to score well in tests or examinations, for example, those from higher socio-economic groups or with well-educated parents, and not select others. If new schools are established, their location is also likely to determine who will apply.

It is also possible that parents from different social groups may be better able to make choices because of their higher levels of education, their ability to access information and their ability to navigate the system. There is also evidence to suggest that different types of parents make choices in different ways (e.g. Flatley et al. 2001; Noden et al. 1998).

Equal access to school can thus be hindered. Moreover, if schools become more segregated greater between-school variance in terms of educational outcomes is likely to follow, having deleterious consequences for equality of opportunity (see West and Nikolai 2013).

### *Access*

#### *Sweden*

It is important to stress that most pupils in Sweden go to the school that is geographically closest to their home. Children can attend a municipal school near to where they live or another school (either a municipal or an independent school). However, there is variation between municipalities in the extent to which parents can choose schools; for example, there is a greater concentration of independent schools in the well-off areas (Båvner et al. 2011).[13]

The decision as to whether or not a pupil should be admitted to a particular school is taken by either the municipality or the independent school. For comprehensive schools owned by the municipality, the main admissions criteria are proximity of the home to the school and siblings. Whilst independent schools must be open to all, if there are more applicants than places available, a number of admissions criteria can be used, namely prioritising siblings already at the school, the time that the child's name has been on the waiting list ('queuing') and proximity to the school (Båvner et al. 2011). Unlike in England, religious schools cannot select on the basis of religion. Thus, there are clear differences in relation to admissions policies in the two countries. Another difference relates to the marketing of schools; in addition to school fairs and advertising, Arreman and Holm (2011) report gifts being offered on enrolment including free driving licences, laptops and journeys abroad, as well as less expensive items such as sweets and pens.

Children with special educational needs may be placed in a certain school by the municipality and an independent school can be requested to admit the child. Whilst the school can decline if the municipality is not paying enough to support the student's needs (Båvner et al. 2011), as a result of the 2010 Education Act, there are now more 'stringent rules on investigation before decisions on admission to schools for children with learning disabilities' not in.

At the upper secondary level, there are different admissions requirements for vocational programmes and those preparing students for higher education (Regeringskansliet 2013);[14] grade-based admission rules can also be used by independent schools (Båvner et al. 2011) and are also used in Stockholm (see Söderström and Uusitalo 2010).

Skolverket (2012) concluded that 'real choice' is not similar for all pupils. Opportunities to choose are affected by the range of schools and programmes at the upper secondary level, where there are academic and vocational programmes (see Alexandersson 2011). When it comes to choice at the upper secondary level, the real choice applies, in the main to those with good grades at the end of compulsory education: 'the pupils with the best grades get their choices' (Skolverket 2012, 15). Other factors include socio-economic background and those with a foreign background. In short:

> although freedom of choice and greater diversity lead to improved chances for parents and pupils to have their wishes and needs met, in practice, the development can lead to reduced choice in some parts of Sweden and for some groups of pupils.

### England

In England, admissions to secondary schools are subject to a mandatory School Admissions Code. Parents/carers must be allowed to express a minimum of three 'choices' (preferences) for publicly-funded schools for their child (see DfE 2012a). They are required to complete a 'common application form' which is provided by and returned to their LA. Schools outside the LA where the child lives can also be named. In some cases, schools are permitted to seek additional information about prospective pupils by asking parents/carers to complete supplementary information forms relating to their specific admissions criteria (e.g. religion in the case of religious schools). In relation to the offer of places, if there are fewer applicants than places available at a particular school, all those expressing a preference must be offered a place for their child (except in the case of grammar schools). If there are more applicants than places, the school's published oversubscription criteria are used to determine which children are offered a place. These typically involve children in public care, distance, siblings and in the case of schools with a religious character, religion (West, Barham, and Hind 2011).

In early March, prior to secondary transfer in September, parents receive an offer from the LA at their 'highest preference school' at which a place is available (DfE 2012b, para. 15). Schools with responsibility for admissions, including academies, have more scope to decide on their admissions criteria than other schools whose admissions policies are set by the LA. Such schools are in a position, if they so wish, to seek to select 'in' and 'out' certain pupils via their oversubscription criteria. For example, selection criteria can include giving priority to a proportion of pupils with aptitude in a particular subject, which is a criterion used by more sponsored academies than other types of publicly-funded schools (West, Barham, and Hind 2011). Admissions to free schools are broadly similar to those of other academies, although they are able to give priority to certain other groups (e.g. children of founding members of the free school trust, children eligible for free school meals) (DfE 2012a).

For converter academies, the criteria used to decide who should be selected in the event of the school being oversubscribed are similar to those of the school from which it converted. Thus, schools that had a religious character pre-conversion are likely to retain admissions criteria designed to test religion, religious denomination or practice. This is significant with respect to segregation: religious schools, including academies, which prioritise in this way, are by definition seeking to affect the school composition.

One group particularly at risk of being disadvantaged in a market environment are those with special educational needs. Children with a 'statement' of special educational needs, carry with them additional resources and if a school (including an academy) is named on the statement (following the agreement of the school governing body) the child must be admitted. For children with no statement, admissions are determined using the standard oversubscription criteria for the school in question. This raises the issue of admissions more generally: admissions arrangements are a key element of the funding agreement between academy trusts (including free schools) and the government. Funding agreements have varied over time. 'Model funding agreements' have been introduced, and since the 2010 Academies Act funding agreements have been less likely to deviate from these model agreements. They include provisions imposing obligations on the academy trust (i.e. owner) equivalent to the special educational needs obligations for maintained schools. Academies are also required to determine admission arrangements in line with requirements in the School Admissions Code. With some more contentious issues, such as pupil exclusions, statute is being used to override parts of funding agreements (Wolfe 2012).

## School composition and segregation

### Sweden

There are differences between the school composition of independent comprehensive schools (*fristående skolor*) and municipality schools, with the former having a larger proportion of girls, a larger proportion of pupils with parents who have continued with education following upper secondary school and a larger proportion of pupils with a foreign background. Further, pupils with a foreign background attending independent comprehensive schools have parents who are better educated than those with a foreign background attending municipal schools (Skolverket 2006). With respect to pupils entitled to tuition in their first language (and tuition in Swedish as a second language) the overall proportions are similar for both municipal and independent comprehensive schools (20% vs. 21%, respectively), but within the latter, significantly higher for religious (48%) than other independent schools (Skolverket 2013).

There have been concerns about increased segregation between pupil backgrounds as a result of the independent school reforms (see Alexandersson 2011). Böhlmark and Lindahl (2007) found some segregation effects as a result of a higher proportion of independent comprehensive schools in a municipality: children of parents who have had more years in education and/or immigrant background were found to be more likely to be sorted into independent schools, as the proportion of independent schools increases. Lindbom (2010) found that the effects of independent schools on school segregation are complex, but concluded that independent schools may have added somewhat to the much more significant effect of increasing residential segregation (see also Båvner et al. 2011; Wiborg 2010). And Östh, Andersson, and Malmberg (2013) argue that the most likely driver of increasing segregation is the rapid transformation of the school system, with parents and pupils increasingly selecting non-neighbourhood schools.

However, the causes of segregation are even more complex due to other policy changes in upper secondary schools. Thus, prior to 2000, in Stockholm, pupils were allocated to their nearest school, but following a policy change that year, pupils could apply to any school within Stockholm and admission decisions were based solely on grades at the end of compulsory school. Söderström and Uusitalo (2010) found that the new admission policy increased segregation by ability, family background and immigration status.

## England

In England, there has been much academic debate about segregation following the introduction of the quasi-market reforms culminating in the 1988 Education Reform Act. Gorard, Hordosy, and See (2013) looked at changes between 1989 and 2011 in segregation across both primary and secondary schools. They found that annual changes in segregation by poverty are not caused by factors that are specific to new types of school that have been introduced (in 2011, 11% of secondary schools were academies). They argue convincingly that the main determinants of segregation in schools are related to residential segregation. There is some evidence to suggest that there were some modest reductions in segregation following legislative changes to limit various forms of social or covert selection (Allen, Coldron, and West 2011).

In terms of school composition, there is evidence demonstrating that some types of schools have more advantaged intakes than others; this is likely to be a result not only of geography and transportation but also of parents' differing choices and different admissions criteria. Thus, academically selective grammar schools admit higher ability children and fewer children eligible for free school meals (an indicator of poverty) (Sutton Trust 2006); and faith schools that are nominally comprehensive have pupil intakes that are of a higher social background and ability than their secular counterparts (Allen and West 2009, 2011).

Turning to academies, there is evidence to suggest that pupil intakes to sponsored secondary academies have changed over time with a year-on-year decrease in the proportion of pupils eligible for free school meals. Thus between 2003 and 2008, the proportion decreased from 45 to 29% (see also Curtis et al. 2008; Hansard 2008). Machin and Vernoit (2011) and Wilson (2011) found that the attainment of pupils entering academies significantly improved after they became sponsored academies with the latter finding that schools that became sponsored academies enrolled approximately 12.5% fewer pupils eligible for free school meals.

This reduction in the proportion of pupils from disadvantaged backgrounds may be because middle-class families consider academies a viable option not having considered their predecessor schools to be so. It may however be argued that the greater ability of the middle classes to 'manoeuvre within the market may disadvantage more socially deprived pupils' (PriceWaterhouseCoopers 2008, 62).

Given that converter academies (the majority of academies) are highly likely to adopt similar admissions criteria to those of the predecessor school on conversion, no specific impact on segregation of *academies* is to be expected at least in the short term, as voluntary schools with a religious character are likely to retain religious admissions criteria once they convert to academies.

## Discussion and comparative analysis

In England and Sweden during the 1980s and 1990s, the school system was subject to the neo-liberal agendas pursued by right of centre governments. In both countries the reforms were continued and expanded by left of centre governments. One of the outcomes was the development of academies in England and independent grant-aided schools in Sweden. Significantly, the idea of free schools – a form of academy – was based not only on the extant CTCs and academies in England but also on the Swedish independent 'free schools'.

The development of the English academies and free schools, and the Swedish independent school programmes varied; to some extent this can be related to their differing histories. In England, the churches have played a significant role in the provision of school-based education and this has continued with the academies programme. In addition, selection by ability, a feature of secondary education in England following the 1944 Education Act has remained with the grammar schools still in existence (grammar schools converting to academy status retain academic selection). Indeed, it might also be argued that quasi-academic selection continued via the selection of a proportion of pupils on the basis of 'aptitude' in subjects such as languages, a feature of sponsored academies under Labour.

In Sweden, a strong version of equality of opportunity, encompassing equal access to schools, has remained a feature even with independent schools: limited admissions criteria to comprehensive independent schools are permitted – distance, siblings and waiting list time. Unlike England, selection on the basis of religion or religious denomination is not permitted.[15] Nevertheless, in practice schools set up by particular religious groups are likely to be chosen by parents and pupils from that group.

The pace of and nature of change in the two countries has differed. In Sweden, fee-charging schools initially converted to become grant-aided independent schools. The number of independent schools has increased slowly and gradually, but there are proportionately more independent upper secondary than comprehensive schools; this is likely to be because it is easier for older pupils to travel to school and so easier for independent school providers to achieve economies of scale.

In England, the academies programme expanded slowly initially. Sponsored academies were first introduced, building on the CTC programme. However, since 2010, following legislation permitting schools to convert to academies, there has been a massive expansion of converter academies. A small but growing number of free schools have been also been established. The process has been one of layering a new institutional form on the existing school system. The changes have been faster than in Sweden, which is likely to be a result of the financial incentives associated with conversion to academy status.

The nature of the privatisation differs between the two countries. In England, although the academy trust – which owns the academy – is a private, non-profit body, in Sweden the majority of independent upper secondary schools are owned by private, for-profit bodies. In England, religious bodies of different types are well represented amongst academy sponsors, and converter academy owners.[16] Whilst there are no for-profit providers, the Conservative Secretary of State for Education, Michael Gove has not ruled out the possibility of for-profit free schools in the future (*The Guardian* 2012).

School composition has been hotly debated in both countries. In Sweden, concerns have been expressed about differences in school composition between independent and municipal schools. In England, concerns have been expressed about changes in the composition of sponsored academies. There are significant concerns relating to increased segregation in both countries, but the segregation is of different types and associated with different factors.

In England, there is no evidence that the academies programme itself has increased segregation. However, religious schools that have converted to academies are perpetuating the segregation associated with schools that have a religious character as a result of their admissions criteria. Geography is important with respect to segregation and although admissions criteria are an element, this is not a function of academy status *per se*. In Sweden, the segregation is tied in with geography and the school choice reforms generally, although recent revelations about independent comprehensive schools selecting pupils on the basis of academic aptitude have led to demands by the opposition Social Democrats for the management of admissions to be taken over by local municipalities (*The Local* 2013). The segregation in upper secondary schools is likely to be associated with the fact that attainment in test results at the end of compulsory school is a key admissions criterion.

Notwithstanding the fact that it is not possible to attribute segregation to the introduction of independent schools in Sweden or academies in England, there is a concern that choice policies may lead to the separation of children into different types of schools, particularly with respect to schools that have a religious profile in Sweden or a religious character (and additionally, religious admissions criteria) in England. In terms of equality of educational opportunity, the issue of segregation is significant. In the Brown vs. Board of Education (1954) case in the USA, it was argued that segregation has the potential to deprive children of 'equal educational opportunities' even though physical facilities and other 'tangible' factors may be equal. In a similar vein it can be argued that segregation arising as a result of school choice policies also has the potential to result in unequal opportunities. A key aspect of education is to 'awaken the child to cultural values' and help him or her to 'adjust normally' to his or her environment (Brown vs. Board of Education 1954) and segregated schooling can deprive children of these influences.[17] And at a societal level, social mixing is likely to be beneficial, not only with regards to pupil performance, but also with regard to social cohesion.

In Sweden, the characteristics of pupils on roll in independent comprehensive schools vary from those in municipality schools; there is also some evidence indicating an increase in segregation at the upper secondary level. In England, there is no evidence of segregation having increased over time. There are however, differences in terms of school composition, particularly with respect to schools with a religious character and grammar schools. The intangible negative consequences of segregation thus remain, and are unlikely to be ameliorated without further policy changes.

The question remains as to whether school owners, who wish to appeal to specific groups of parents or pupils – for example, those from particular social or religious groups – are likely to take note of exhortations to reduce segregation, especially if these conflict with either their own mission (as in the case of religious schools) or their income stream and popularity (in the case of for-profit providers). In short, privatisation, diversity, choice and school autonomy seem unlikely to address policy concerns surrounding reducing segregation and increasing social cohesion.

## Acknowledgements

I would like to thank the Swedish officials who agreed to be interviewed: this paper has benefited enormously from their contributions. Thanks also to Elizabeth Bailey, Audrey Hind, Philip Noden, Mikael Alexandersson and Ian Craig for their assistance.

## Notes

1. The school leaving age increased to 16 in 1972. From 2015, participation in education and training will be compulsory until 18.
2. Church schools could opt for increased state funding and control by local education authorities (LEAs) as 'voluntary-controlled schools' or reduced state support and more independence (including control over pupil admissions) as 'voluntary-aided schools' (see Allen and West 2011).
3. Very few technical schools were introduced (Gordon, Aldrich, and Dean 1991).
4. Alexandersson (2011) identifies three dimensions to the notion of equivalence: entry (equal access to schooling), stay (equal learning opportunities in school) and exit (equal academic and social outcomes). These three elements are similar to those identified with respect to 'equality of opportunity' (see West and Nikolai 2013).
5. If a proposition is passed it results in an amendment to the relevant piece of legislation, in this case the Education Act 1985:1100.
6. Schools owned by corporations or stock market companies are vulnerable to the vagaries of the market and closure: e.g. in 2013, JB Education decided to sell 19 of its high schools and close down eight others: this was because the Danish private equity group Axcel, which bought the chain in 2008, decided it could no longer continue to cover the company's losses (*The Guardian* 2013).
7. In England, around 7% of children attend fee-charging independent schools, some of which were historically known as 'public schools'.
8. The School Standards and Framework Act 1998 abolished grant-maintained status: schools were designated as one of three new types of school – community, voluntary (aided and controlled) and foundation. Grant-maintained schools became, in the main, foundation schools with schools that had previously been voluntarily returning to voluntary status.
9. Following the 2000 Learning and Skills Act and the 2002 Education Act.
10. CTCs also started converting to academies.
11. As are other school types including CTCs and voluntary schools (see West and Bailey 2013).
12. Prior to 1 April 2009 LEAs were the bodies responsible for the local administration of state sector education services. The statutory duties of LEAs are now undertaken by the Director of Children's Services within each Local Authority district (ONS 2013).
13. Lubienski (2013) note that in the US many charter schools, especially those for profit avoid areas with the highest need.
14. Pupils who have completed their final year of compulsory education and have pass grades in Swedish/Swedish as a second language, English, mathematics and at least five other subjects can apply for upper secondary school vocational programmes; pupils must have a pass grade in at least nine subjects in addition to Swedish, English and mathematics (Regeringskansliet 2013).
15. According to the 2010 Education Act 'The teaching at independent schools … must be non-confessional. The education in more general terms at independent schools … may have a confessional orientation. The participation in confessional elements must be voluntary'.
16. Whilst Tony Blair was Prime Minister, there was a strong encouragement of religious schools (Walford 2008).
17. For example, in one study pupils from minority groups attending segregated schools expressed a desire to know if they were speaking 'proper' Swedish or behaving 'properly', which they felt that daily contact with ethnic Swedish pupils could provide (see Bunar 2010).

# References

Alexandersson, M. 2011. "Equivalence and Choice in Combination: The Swedish Dilemma." *Oxford Review of Education* 37 (2): 195–214.

Allen, R., J. Coldron, and A. West. 2011. "The Effect of Changes in Published Secondary School Admissions on Pupil Composition." *Journal of Education Policy* 27 (3): 349–366.

Allen, R., and A. West. 2009. "Religious Schools in London: School Admissions, Religious Composition and Selectivity." *Oxford Review of Education* 35 (4): 471–494.

Allen, R., and A. West. 2011. "Why do Faith Secondary Schools have Advantaged Intakes? The Relative Importance of Neighbourhood Characteristics, Social Background and Religious Identification amongst Parents." *British Educational Research Journal* 37 (4): 691–712.

Arreman, I. E., and A.-S. Holm. 2011. "Privatisation of Public Education? The Emergence of Independent Upper Secondary Schools in Sweden." *Journal of Education Policy* 26 (2): 225–243.

Ask, B. 1992. "Freedom of Choice and Independent Schools: A Speech by the Government's School Minister." In *Choice and the Use of Market Forces in Schooling: Swedish Education Reforms in the 1990s*, edited by G. Miron, 101–105. Stockholm: Institute of International Education, Stockholm University.

Bassett, D., G. Lyon, W. Tanner, and B. Watkin. 2012. *Plan A+ Unleashing the Potential of Academies*. London: The Schools Network and Reform.

Båvner, P., A. Barklund, A. Hellewell, and M. Svensson. 2011. *OECD – Overcoming School Failure. Country Background Report Sweden*. Stockholm: Ministry of Education and Research, Government Offices of Sweden. http://www.oecd.org/sweden/49528267.pdf.

Blomqvist, P. 2004. "The Choice Revolution: Privatization of Swedish Welfare Services in the 1990s." *Social Policy and Administration* 38 (2): 139–155.

Böhlmark, A., and M. Lindahl. 2007. *The Impact of School Choice on Pupil Achievement, Segregation and Costs: Swedish Evidence*. Discussion Paper No. 2786. Bonn: Institute for the Study of Labor.

Brown vs. Board of Education, 347 U.S. 483. 1954. *(USSC+) Supreme Court of the United States*. http://www.nationalcenter.org/brown.html.

Bunar, N. 2010. "Choosing for Quality or Inequality: Current Perspectives on the Implementation of School Choice Policy in Sweden." *Journal of Education Policy* 25 (1): 1–18.

Curtis, A., S. Exley, A. Sasia, S. Tough, and G. Whitty. 2008. *The Academies Programme: Progress, Problems and Possibilities*. London: The Sutton Trust.

Department for Education and Skills. 2005. *Higher Standards Better Schools for All*. Cm 6677. London: The Stationery Office. http://publications.education.gov.uk/eOrderingDownload/Cm%206677.pdf.pdf.

Department for Education/Welsh Office. 1992. *Choice and Diversity: A New Framework for Schools*. Cm 2021. London: HMSO.

DfE (Department for Education). 2010. *The Importance of Teaching*. Cm 7980. London: HMSO.

DfE. 2012a. *School Admissions Code*. London: DfE.

DfE. 2012b. *Schools, Pupils and Their Characteristics: January 2012*. London: DfE. Table 2b. https://www.gov.uk/government/publications/schools-pupils-and-their-characteristics-january-2012.

DfE. 2013a. *University Technical Colleges and Studio Schools*. http://www.education.gov.uk/schools/leadership/typesofschools/technical.

DfE. 2013b. *Schools, Pupils and Their Characteristics: January 2013*. London: DfE. Table 2b and 2c. https://www.gov.uk/government/publications/schools-pupils-and-their-characteristics-january-2013.

DfE. 2013c. *Schools, Open Academies and Academy Projects in Development.* http://www.edu-cation.gov.uk/schools/leadership/typesofschools/academies/b00208569/open-academies.

DfE. 2013d. *Open Free Schools.* http://www.education.gov.uk/schools/leadership/type-sofschools/freeschools/b00222175/open.

Ellingsaeter, A. L., and A. Leira. 2006. "Epilogue: Scandinavian Policies of Parenthood – A Success Story?" In *Politicising Parenthood in Scandinavia: Gender Relations in Welfare States*, edited by A. L. Ellingsaeter and A. Leira, 265–278. Bristol: Policy Press.

Eurypedia. 2013. *Sweden: Organisation of Private Education.* https://webgate.ec.europa.eu/fpfis/mwikis/eurydice/index.php/Sweden:Organisation_of_Private_Education.

Fägerlind, I., and L. J. Saha. 1989. *Education and National Development.* London: Pergamon Press.

Flatley, J., H. Connolly, V. Higgins, J. Williams, J. Coldron, K. Stephenson, A. Logie, and N. Smith. 2001. *Parents' Experiences of the Process of Choosing a Secondary School.* Research Report 278. London: DfES.

Gorard, S. 2009. "What Are Academies the Answer to?" *Journal of Education Policy* 24 (1): 101–113.

Gorard, S., R. Hordosy, and B. H. See. 2013. "Narrowing down the Determinants of between-school Segregation: An Analysis of the Intake to All Schools in England, 1989–2011." *Journal of School Choice* 7 (2): 182–195.

Gordon, P., R. Aldrich, and D. Dean. 1991. *Education and Policy in England in the Twenti-eth Century.* London: The Woburn Press.

Gov.uk. 2013. *Setting up a Free School.* https://www.gov.uk/set-up-free-school.

Green, A., J. Preston, and J. G. Janmaat. 2006. *Education, Equality and Social Cohesion.* London: Palgrave.

Hansard. 2008. *Parliamentary Answer by Jim Knight*, October 9, Column 806W. http://www.publications.parliament.uk/pa/cm200708/cmhansrd/cm081009/text/81009w0020.htm#08100960000073.

Harvey, D. 2005. *A Brief History of Neoliberalism.* Oxford: Oxford University Press.

Hursh, D. 2007. "Assessing No Child Left behind and the Rise of Neoliberal Education Policies." *American Educational Research Journal* 44 (3): 493–518.

Husén, T. 1986. "Why Did Sweden Go Comprehensive?" *Oxford Review of Education* 12 (2): 153–163.

Klitgaard, M. B. 2009. "Agenda Setting and Political Institutions in Education Policy: A Cross Country Comparison." In *Governance of Welfare State Reform: A Cross National and Cross Sectoral Comparison of Policy and Politics*, edited by I. Dingeldey and H. Rothgang, 219–237. Cheltenham: Edward Elgar.

Le Grand, J., and W. Bartlett, eds. 1993. *Quasi-markets and Social Policy.* London: Macmillan.

Lindbom, A. 2010. "School Choice in Sweden: Effects on Student Performance, School Costs, and Segregation." *Scandinavian Journal of Educational Research* 54 (6): 615–630.

Lubienski, C. 2013. "Privatising Form or Function? Equity, Outcomes and Influence in American Charter Schools." *Oxford Review of Education* 39 (4): 498–513.

Lundahl, L. 2002. "Sweden: Decentralization, Deregulation, Quasi-markets – And Then What?" *Journal of Education Policy* 17 (6): 687–697.

Lundahl, L. 2005. "A Matter of Self-governance and Control." *European Education* 37 (1): 10–25.

Lundqvist, L. J. 1988. "Privatization: Towards a Concept for Comparative Policy Analysis." *Journal of Public Policy* 8 (1): 1–19.

Machin, S., and J. Vernoit. 2011. *Changing School Autonomy: Academy Schools and Their Introduction to England's Education.* London: CEP, LSE.

Miron, G. 1993. *Choice and the Use of Market Forces in Schooling: Swedish Education Reforms in the 1990s.* Stockholm: Institute of International Education, Stockholm University.

National Audit Office. 2010. *The Academies Programme.* London: NAO.

Noden, P., A. West, M. David, and A. Edge. 1998. "Choices and Destinations at Transfer to Secondary Schools in London." *Journal of Education Policy* 13 (2): 221–236.

ONS. 2013. *Local Education Authorities (LEAs)/Education and Library Boards.* http://www.ons.gov.uk/ons/guide-method/geography/beginner-s-guide/other/local-education-authorities/index.html.

Östh, J., E. Andersson, and B. Malmberg. 2013. "School Choice and Increasing Performance Difference: A Counterfactual Approach." *Urban Studies* 50 (2): 407–425.

Power, S., and C. Taylor. 2013. "Social Justice and Education in the Public and Private Spheres." *Oxford Review of Education* 39 (4): 464–479.

PriceWaterhouseCoopers. 2008. *Academies Evaluation Fifth Annual Report*. London: DCSF.

Regeringskansliet (Government Offices of Sweden). 2009. *An Education Act for Knowledge, Choice and Security*. July 1, 2009. http://www.skolverket.se/sb/d/355.

Regeringskansliet. 2013. *Upper Secondary School*. http://www.government.se/sb/d/10485.

Silver, H. 1973. "Introduction." In *Equal Opportunities in Education*, edited by H. Silver, xi–xxvi. London: Methuen.

Simon, B. 1991. *Education and the Social Order*. London: Lawrence and Wishart.

Skolinspektionen. 2013. *Unpublished Database of Independent School Providers*.

Skolverket. 2004. *Descriptive Data on Childcare, Schools and Adult Education in Sweden 2003*, 34, 35, 38. Stockholm: Skolverket.

Skolverket. 2005. *Children, Pupils and Staff – National Level*. Part 2, 2005. Table 3.1A, p. 82, 6.1A, p. 147.

Skolverket. 2006. *Schools like Any Other? Independent Schools as Part of the System 1991–2004*. Stockholm: Skloverket.

Skolverket. 2010. *Children, Pupils and Staff – National Level*. Part 2, 2009. Table 2A, p. 94, Table 2A, p. 191.

Skolverket. 2012. *Mapping the School Market*. Stockholm: Skolverket.

Skolverket. 2013. *Barn, elever och personal Riksnivå* [Children, Pupils and Staff National Level], *2013*. Rapport 388. Stockholm: Skolveket. Tabell 2A, p. 93, Tabell 4 A, p. 179. http://www.skolverket.se/om-skolverket/visa-enskild-publikation?_xurl_=http%3A%2F%2Fwww5.skolverket.se%2Fwtpub%2Fws%2Fskolbok%2Fwpubext%2Ftrycksak%2FRecord%3Fk%3D3023.

Söderström, M., and R. Uusitalo. 2010. "School Choice and Segregation: Evidence from an Admission Reform." *Scandinavian Journal of Economics* 112: 55–76.

Sutton Trust. 2006. *The Social Composition of Top Comprehensive Schools*. London: The Sutton Trust.

*The Guardian*. 2012. "Michael Gove Open-minded over State Schools Being Run for Profit." May 29. http://www.theguardian.com/politics/2012/may/29/michael-gove-open-state-schools-profit.

*The Guardian*. 2013. "Swedish Free School Operator to Close, Leaving Hundreds of Pupils Stranded." May 31. http://www.guardian.co.uk/education/2013/may/31/free-schools-education.

*The Local*. 2013. "Remove Free School Admission Rights: Löfven." November 2. http://www.thelocal.se/20131102/remove-free-school-admission-rights-social-democrats.

Walford, G. 2000. "From City Technology Colleges to Sponsored Grant-maintained Schools." *Oxford Review of Education* 26 (2): 145–158.

Walford, G. 2008. "Faith-based Schools in England after Ten Years of Tony Blair." *Oxford Review of Education* 34 (6): 689–699.

West, A., and E. Bailey. 2013. "The Development of the Academies Programme: 'Privatising' School-based Education in England 1986–2013." *British Journal of Educational Studies* 61 (2): 137–159.

West, A., E. Barham, and A. Hind. 2011. "Secondary School Admissions in England 2001 to 2008: Changing Legislation, Policy and Practice." *Oxford Review of Education* 37 (1): 1–20.

West, A., and R. Nikolai. 2013. "Welfare Regimes and Education Regimes: Equality of Opportunity and Expenditure in the EU (and US)." *Journal of Social Policy* 42: 469–493.

Whitty, G., A. Edwards, and S. Gewirtz. 1993. *Specialisation and Choice in Urban Education: The City Technology College Experiment*. London: Routledge.

Wiborg, S. 2010. *Swedish Free Schools: Do They Work?* LLAKES Research Paper 18. London: LLAKES.

Wilson, J. 2011. *Are England's Academies More Inclusive or More 'Exclusive'? The Impact of Institutional Change on the Pupil Profile of Schools*. CEE Discussion Paper 125. London: LSE.

Wolfe, D. 2012. *Funding Agreements to Be Overridden by Statute*. http://davidwolfe.org.uk/wordpress/archives/1245.

Zimmer, R., B. Gill, K. Booker, S. Lavertu, T. Sass, and J. Witte. 2009. *Charter Schools in Eight States: Effects on Achievement, Attainment, Integration, and Competition*. Santa Monica, CA: RAND Corporation. http://www.rand.org/pubs/monographs/MG869.

## Appendix 1

**Table A1. Number of comprehensive schools in Sweden by type.**

| Year | All independent schools[*] | Municipal schools[**] | All publicly funded secondary schools |
|------|------|------|------|
| 1998/99 | 331 | 4661 | 4992 |
| 1999/00 | 371 | 4677 | 5048 |
| 2000/01 | 428 | 4662 | 5090 |
| 2001/02 | 485 | 4590 | 5075 |
| 2002/03 | 538 | 4571 | 5109 |
| 2003/04 | 565 | 4476 | 5041 |
| 2004/05 | 576 | 4387 | 4963 |
| 2005/06 | 596 | 4312 | 4908 |
| 2006/07 | 610 | 4262 | 4872 |
| 2007/08 | 635 | 4191 | 4826 |
| 2008/09 | 677 | 4078 | 4755 |
| 2009/10 | 709 | 3951 | 4660 |
| 2010/11 | 741 | 3885 | 4626 |
| 2011/12 | 761 | 3855 | 4616 |
| 2012/13 | 790 | 4119 | 4909 |

[*]Includes international and national boarding schools.
[**]Includes Sami schools ($N = 5$–6).
Source: Skolverket (2004, 2005, 2010, 2013).

**Table A2. Number of upper secondary schools in Sweden by type.**

| Year | All independent schools | Municipal and county council schools | All secondary schools |
|------|------|------|------|
| 1996/97 | 77 | 564 | 641 |
| 1997/98 | 82 | 556 | 638 |
| 1998/99 | 86 | 538 | 624 |
| 1999/00 | 107 | 489 | 596 |
| 2000/01 | 135 | 519 | 654 |
| 2001/02 | 148 | 506 | 654 |
| 2002/03 | 200 | 517 | 717 |
| 2003/04 | 241 | 515 | 756 |
| 2004/05 | 247 | 516 | 763 |
| 2005/06 | 272 | 523 | 795 |
| 2006/07 | 300 | 518 | 818 |
| 2007/08 | 359 | 530 | 889 |
| 2008/09 | 414 | 531 | 945 |
| 2009/10 | 458 | 518 | 976 |
| 2010/11 | 489 | 526 | 1015 |
| 2011/12 | 499 | 506 | 1005 |
| 2012/13 | 485 | 768 | 1253 |

Sources: Skolverket (2005, 2010, 2013).

**Table A3. Numbers of secondary schools in England by type January 2002–January 2013.**

| Year (January) | CTCs | Secondary sponsored academies | Secondary converter academies | Free schools, UTC and studio schools | LA secondary schools | All publicly funded secondary schools |
|---|---|---|---|---|---|---|
| 2001/02 | 14 | 0 | | | 3457 | 3471 |
| 2002/03 | 15 | 3 | | | 3436 | 3454 |
| 2003/04 | 14 | 12 | | | 3409 | 3435 |
| 2004/05 | 14 | 17 | | | 3385 | 3416 |
| 2005/06 | 11 | 27 | | | 3367 | 3405 |
| 2006/07 | 10 | 46 | | | 3343 | 3399 |
| 2007/08 | 5 | 83 | | | 3295 | 3383 |
| 2008/09 | 3 | 133 | | | 3225 | 3361 |
| 2009/10 | 3 | 203 | | | 3127 | 3333 |
| 2010/11 | 3 | 271 | 100 | | 2936 | 3310 |
| 2011/12 | 3 | 330 | 827 | 6 | 2102 | 3268 |
| 2012/13 | 3 | 401 | 1187 | 50 | 1640 | 3281 |

Sources: West and Bailey (2013) and DfE (2012b, 2013b).

# Setting up a free school: successful proposers' experiences

Paul Miller, Barrie Craven and James Tooley

*E.G. West Centre, Newcastle University, Newcastle upon Tyne, UK*

The 2010 Academies Act was significant in introducing Free Schools to the English education system. Opening up funding to new, non-profit entrants on the basis of demand, the policy has aroused support and controversy on political, philosophical and practical educational grounds with implications for social justice in terms of equity and freedom. Given the ostensible quality and empowerment goals of the enacted new (limited) freedoms, the extent of activity towards them is evaluated alongside the Department for Education application procedure's fitness for purpose. Opinions and experiences of free school proposers were gathered through four in-depth interviews and a wider questionnaire yielding data from 19 of 55 successful proposers opening schools in September 2012. Wider policy issues are considered, notably concerning concepts of social justice. While successful applicants appeared to meet the policy's demand and educational quality prerequisites, procedural uncertainties and inefficiencies hampered their progress. Furthermore, political and philosophical opposition and practical limits to time, expertise and resources have constrained the policy's systemic impact. Regarding social justice, whether Free Schools enhance choice or reduce equity remains largely a moot point given the obstacles to system-wide change.

## 1. Introduction

Introduced in the 2010 Academies Act, the UK Conservative/Liberal Democrat Coalition Government's Free School policy encourages diverse organisations to initiate new schools in England. Independent of Local Authorities (LAs), they are financed centrally on the per capita basis applied to LA-maintained schools (DfE 2013b). Free Schools' distinction from Academies (introduced under the previous Labour Government) owes to their status as 'Additional Schools' (Academies Act 2010, 6). This would include instances where an Academy is set up in place of a previous maintained school and subsequently provides for a greater age range.

Although private schools have long trickled into the English state education system, the 2010 Academies Act purposefully sought to increase the regulated new entry of organisations therein. As such, the initiative promotes the establishment of schools in areas with a perceived local demand. According to the Coalition Government:

> Free Schools are all-ability state-funded schools set up in response to what local people say they want and need in order to improve education for children in their community. (DfE 2013a)

This paper examines the Free School application experiences of some of the 55 Free Schools opened in September 2012 and reports on detailed interviews with four successful applicants opening schools in 2012 and 2013. The primacy of proposers' perspectives is considered apt given this Department for Education (DfE) claim:

> it is now much easier for talented and committed teachers, charities, parents and education experts to open schools to address real demand within an area. (DfE 2013a)

Analysis of proposers' motivation and activity, support received, opposition faced and overall application experience allows an evaluation of efforts towards the policy's ostensible aim: empowering groups interested in improving education. It was found that despite securing unambiguous support from prospective pupils' parents, the responding Free Schools' proposers often faced opposition from local politicians, councillors and other schools. In the context of contemporary educational debates, the paper concludes that, given the practical hurdles experienced, the application process may have been unnecessarily onerous, time-consuming and inconsistent. Appropriate procedural streamlining, standardisation and transparency alongside provision for pertinent proposal support would have facilitated greater action toward promoting the policy's stated aims by assisting virtuous but resource-strapped applications. The subsequent evolution of procedures is briefly evaluated before recommendations for policy development and future research are made, with implications for social justice considered.

Depending on the perspective taken, the Free School policy's realisation in action can be seen to promote or hinder achieving concepts of Social Justice. In ostensibly promoting parental choice, it could be aligned with comparative perspectives supporting a plurality of preferred, but imperfect, outcomes as espoused by Sen (2009). Given long-term State retreat from education, were reality to match rhetoric, a matured policy might lead to parents increasingly exercising choice in their children's education, affecting equality and freedom concepts at individual and structural levels. However, practical and imposed policy constraints currently limit extensive Social Justice considerations regarding both the policy's procedures and likely outcomes.

## 2. Literature review

### 2.1. The Nature of free schools and the application process

The Education Funding Agency (EFA) centrally finances Free Schools per capita, with each pupil attracting the same sum as LA schools (DfE 2013b). Additional, unspecified capital grants are available for buildings, IT infrastructure and furniture, with an emphasis on 'value for money' (NSN). Accountability is purportedly derived through a funding agreement signed with the Government, with the DfE and Ofsted monitoring performance. LAs coordinate pupil admissions (DfE 2013b), although unlike maintained schools, Free Schools (like Academies) manage their staffing independently and can diverge from the National Curriculum provided Maths, English and Science are taught in a broad, balanced curriculum. Therefore, the 'freeness' implied in their name relates to curriculum and staffing, and cost at the point of delivery to parents.

Free School proposals are vetted for approval in an iterative, DfE-run process. This and the success criteria for schools opening in 2012 and 2013 were continually and opaquely developed and refined and, therefore, not described here fully. An idealised version for schools opening in September 2014, below (Figure 1), is mildly indicative, although the reality of associated procedures, e.g. for funding agreements, was considerably more complex.

For 2012 and 2013 applicants, the process included successive proposal and business case stages, the latter requiring demonstration of parental demand for the proposed provision. For Free Schools opening in 2015, the process and criteria have evolved further with three staggered application rounds and two different 'routes', including a stripped down process for current Free Schools setting up further, similar schools.

## 2.2. Participants in the process

There are two key bodies involved with assessing, assisting and implementing the process. These are: the DfE, centrally responsible for the whole process including application criteria and approval, and the New Schools Network (NSN). Founded by Rachel Wolf (ex-advisor to the Conservative Minister for Education, Michael Gove), this charity was funded with an initial £500,000 Government grant (Hatcher 2011, 488) and provides advice and development guidance to groups setting up Free Schools.

## 2.3. Early experiences

The originator of the first Free School, Toby Young (2012), described a complex original process as a shifting 'bureaucratic labyrinth' (65), with evolving legal and

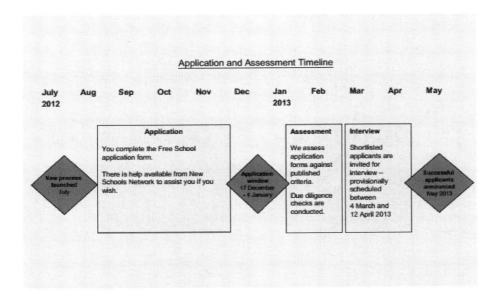

Figure 1.  2014 Free School Application and Assessment Timeline (DfE 2012).

regulatory frameworks causing misunderstanding and disagreement, even within the DfE itself. Young further outlined the practical difficulties of working as volunteers:

> (y)ou cannot tell someone who is not being paid to have Ealing Council's Pupil Place Planning projections for 2010–2020 on your desk first thing tomorrow morning. You have to do it yourself. (66)

Young expressed the continued ability of LAs to 'make things difficult for volunteer groups like mine' despite the Free School policy removing their veto on new schools. A problematic backdrop is described, including issues securing a building as a charitable trust and likely opposition from 'teaching unions … as well as other ideologically hostile groups' (64) towards employing an experienced management company.

## 2.4. Academic and political debate

Allowing Free Schools as additional Academies is complex when viewed through their political (Hatcher 2011; Whitty and Power 2000), historical (Walford 2000) and cultural (Chapman and Salokangas 2012) contexts. The latter academics classify Free Schools (and Academies) as 'Independent state-funded schools' (ISFS) given their central public funding under diverse strategic management executive control. Groups and chains of ISFS form part of a general (small-scale thus far) systemic change in education from 'public sector monopoly' towards something more 'messy, patchy and diverse' (Ball 2012, 100). Chapman and Salokangas (2012) propose engendering an egalitarian culture to effect whole system improvement. However, evolutionary and managed change (Schein 2010) desired by parents, children and teachers may be more feasible within loose or tight federations given proximity to 'the values and beliefs of the participants' (Bush 1995, 138) and individualised UK group culture (Chapman and Salokangas 2012, 478).

Given the perceived disruptive potential of Free Schools' introduction (following Academies), related ideological differences underscore lively academic debate in England (Allen and Burgess 2011a; Croft 2011; Hatcher 2011; Wright 2012; Young 2012), predictably reflected in the national media according to traditional political stance. By actively 'encouraging new providers – including new alternative provision Free Schools' (DfE 2010, 33), the policy is associated with issues of quality, social justice and the respective responsibilities of parents and state towards the education of children (Croft 2011; Wright 2012). Hopes for (Croft 2011; Young 2012) and fears of (Hatcher 2011) an increased role for the profit motive in the UK education system are contiguous.

In the context of the 'very classical liberal' debate over 'the role of individual as against state responsibilities' (Ball 2012, 101) being played out, Hatcher (2011) sees concordance across the political spectrum of the UK's three main political parties, lending credence to Ball's portrayal of a 'reluctant state' (2012). Hultin summarises the current balance of power thus:

> We are witnessing a significant migration of schools from state control to independence and from state ownership to … private … the purpose … to capture the 'good' side of the market, i.e. introducing choice and diversity, while protecting schools and pupils from … the profit motive. (2012, 147)

Nevertheless, per Young (2012), opposition from LAs follows from an attendant reduction in funding and control. Although Hatcher (2011, 501) intimates Free Schools' independence from LAs as a threat to democracy, adherents to Buchanan's 'politics without romance' (2003) of public choice theory may consider this rather to represent self-preservation.

### 2.5. Investment and profits

Given limited Government budgets and (therefore) potential for systemic change, commentators have suggested emboldening the Free School initiative by allowing profit-making companies to open schools. Associated innovation and efficient investment are cited alongside an imperative to satisfy customers (Stanfield 2012) by providing 'good' quality education (Bergstrom 2012, 93; Tooley 2000). While attendant expansion of '"competitive threat" to underperforming local schools' may drive potential for 'pedagogical innovation' (Allen and Burgess 2011b), fears of 'profiteering' exist (Wright 2012, 282). Presently, UK politicians either concur with the latter or predict unpopularity among the electorate (Hatcher 2011). Despite profitmaking pervading other elements of education (Ball 2012; Stanfield 2012), the polemic around opening Free School applications to profitmaking organisations belies underlying philosophical tensions.

### 2.6. Social justice and free schools

The Free School policy can, therefore, inspire differing reactions regarding social justice, depending on views held on optimal approaches to, and/or outcomes of, the concept. Those favouring the singularly conceived and structured Rawlsian approach (1971) might look to guarantee social justice through equalised zonal state provision under ideal structures, protecting the significant number of pupils whose parents cannot afford, or do not desire, to pay expensive school fees or move house to exercise school choice. Tooley (2013) prefers (and argues in the developing world context) that social justice can rather be achieved under Sen's pluralistic vision via a system of increased (private) school choice. However, Walford cites legitimate concerns (as will occur (Sen 2009, 15) with imperfect rather than ultimate solutions based on plural comparisons and decisions) over those least able to make choices (Walford 2006, 199).

In word (and to be seen whether in deed), the Free School policy aims to redress social injustice at least by enhancing families' recourse to their desired schooling, although children with parents unable, unwilling or incompetent at making these choices might suffer through diverted resources and reduced collective parental voice and peer diversity. Beyond the procedural necessity to demonstrate evidence of demand, political pronouncements seek to account for this, laying 'claim to a politics of redistribution' (Power and Taylor 2013, 467) by, outwardly at least, encouraging and highlighting proposals targeting the most deprived (Conservative Party).

The ready availability of alternatives intended by the policy is likely, in the short term, to remain limited in scale (Allen and Burgess 2011a) and scope due to limited central finance and central governance effecting superficiality of choice (Walford 2006, 206). Whether this is achieved in the long term depends on the policy's future evolution. If taken to scale, equality of educational opportunity would depend more explicitly on parents' basis for, and ability in, making choices, potentially enhanced by increased onus for them to consider educational options. Interested parties would be incentivised to provide information, notwithstanding any opportunistic short-term tactics to misinform.

The Free School Policy, as a recent addition to the contemporary educational landscape in England, could potentially fit with Sen's comparative approach to justice (2009) depending on the extent of its realisation in practice. The nature of the new schools founded and the process they have undergone are explored with this context in mind. Whether overall 'user democracy' is enhanced as intimated by Government descriptions (DfE 2013a), or whether systemic restrictions exist, our focus follows Sergiovanni (2003) in being situated closer to the demands of the actors involved, or 'the purposes, values and beliefs of parents, teachers and students' (18). As such the 'lifeworld might drive the systemsworld' (16) from the ground level. Since little research exists regarding proposers' motives, efforts and experiences, this focus can potentially indicate beneficial proposer actions towards meeting educational needs. Obstacles to facilitating this end may also be highlighted and appropriate procedural improvements suggested.

## 3.  Methodology

### 3.1.  *Research purpose, design and strategy*

This study explores and evaluates proposer accounts and opinion of Free School application experiences, in accordance with Sen's acceptance of possible plural definitions of social justice, positioning it close to individual and community levels (Sergiovanni 2003, 23) of social groups involved. A pragmatic approach led to the iterative and complementary use of mixed methods. In-depth interviews with four successful Free School applications scheduled to open across 2012 and 2013 provided depth of evidence, with themes further explored using a cross-sectional survey to enhance generalisation with limited quantitative and qualitative analysis. To extend evaluation of the policy to the English national level, questionnaires were sent to all 55 successful applications for Free Schools opening in 2013. Nineteen completed questionnaires were returned (35%). The research process outline was as follows.

### 3.2.  *Research stage 1 – interviews*

The main proposers of four distinctive and purposively selected, successful Free School applications were interviewed. The applications were at various stages of the process. Interviews occurred separately between 4 and 25 July 2012. Two researchers (an educationalist and an economist) were present.

Following a review of relevant contemporary issues and initial conversations with Free School applicants, semi-structured interviews attempted to illuminate proposer motivation for setting up the schools and experiences of the official process. It was felt (correctly) that employing open discussion questions making reference to certain areas would be likely to sufficiently cover identified themes while allowing interviewees considerable control over the interview direction. Backup interview protocols ensured full coverage of relevant internal and external issues. The schools involved were anonymised as agreed. Further synthesis was then undertaken following completion of all interviews, forming the 'Discussion' section subsequent to the research findings.

## 3.3. Research stage 2 – questionnaires

Questionnaires were produced to further develop the themes revealed in the content of the interviews and included several open questions to allow for potentially multiple perspectives. This mitigated the danger of any specific issues present in the schools participating at the interview stage being given undue emphasis.

The questionnaire was distributed, in early November 2012, to the principal Proposers of all 55 Free Schools opening in September 2012, with a response rate of 35%. No obvious response bias could be inferred given the small numbers regarding geographical split, religious designation and Free School type (primary, secondary, all through or special/alternative).

## 3.4. Limitations

Limited resources and a desire to focus investigations meant that unsuccessful proposals were not included. Future studies could perhaps be usefully expanded to take account of these.

Despite the potential for the small research population to cause participant fear of identification (even after guarantees of anonymity), there was no evidence of questionnaire respondents holding back on opinion.

The study is frozen in time and therefore somewhat historical. Given the recentness of the Act, future modifications are likely; indeed refined guidelines published in June 2013 (DfE 2013c) mean that experiences and opinions concern an already revised process. Nevertheless, this study can yield important learning, in particular via its practitioner focus, such that future application procedures may be usefully evaluated.

## 4. Findings

The presentation of mini-case findings is roughly structured by proposer motivation, effort and experience.

## 4.1. Research stage 1 – mini case findings

Diverse characteristics, motivations and experiences of application are represented in the four Free Schools' evidence. These are partly influenced by variations in application origins and immediate local circumstances and councils. Nevertheless common themes emerged, including heavy bureaucracy regarding paperwork and time spent on application procedures, suggesting that the (necessary) procedure to ensure legitimate and efficient use of tax monies is not optimal. In Section 4.2.4 a more complex situation than mere resentment of careful administration is uncovered. Findings are presented case by case below.

### 4.1.1. Case 1 (School A)

*4.1.1.1. Proposer motivation and efforts.* The first case involved the conversion of a fee-paying independent school to a Free School. Being unusually located in one of the most deprived communities nationally was an important factor in the application's ultimately positive evaluation. By 2010 the school was feeling the financial effects of the prolonged economic downturn; bad and doubtful debts were rising, discounted fees were given to siblings and scholarships were being used to entice pupils. Thus, financial pressures were a major factor in the application with clear benefits to Free School conversion. Although per capita Local Authority awards were less than private fees, the gap was unproblematic since there would be no discounts, no free scholarships or empty places. Additionally, Free School conversion supported the founders' original school vision 20 years previously; to provide a quality, affordable education for low-income families.

Demand for the Free School was determined by staff distribution of questionnaires and leaflets. Seven hundred completed questionnaires were returned or collected, of which two school cleaners were responsible for collecting 250! Responses were massively favourable. At the time of interview, the school had 190 applications for 40 places in September 2012. Selection based on children currently in care, on siblings of current pupils and then distance from school, would, over time, narrow the catchment area toward the school's immediate (socially deprived) radius. Anecdotally, instances of low-income parents raiding savings and borrowing to afford one year of fees without guarantees that Free School status would be granted represented considerable calculated risks to ensure their children's admission *despite* long-term inability to afford fees.

*4.1.1.2. Support, opposition and process.* All but one set of the school's pupils' parents were reported to be in favour of conversion. Mixed reactions to proposals came from Head Teachers of nearby schools, with concern over losing pupils to the new Free School. Some strong political opposition came from some within Unions and Councils. One such individual, while personally in favour of anticipated benefits for a deprived area, was politically against. Within the school, the success of the Free School application was credited to its potentially positive impact in this area. Nevertheless the application process was reportedly a 'very rocky road'.

### 4.1.2. Case 2 (School B)

*4.1.2.1. Proposer motivation and efforts.* The proposers, a charity, had identified problems facing them through dialogue with families and finding how education had 'failed' both parents and children. Considerable local charitable work underpinned an awareness of a strong need for alternative and improved educational offerings and engaging families in education. The trustees believed a fresh start was needed beyond adapting current schools. Therefore, the school would only accept pupils new to school, meaning a Reception class entry level. The proposers also recognised the necessity for parental support and to reach children early, before formal schooling. By knocking on doors, proposers gathered over 100 parents of children aged 3½ years on a mailing list, with 70 committing their children to the school, despite not yet having secured a site.

*4.1.2.2. Support, opposition and process.* A lack of trust ('them and us') and opposition, in principle, came from other charities, teachers, schools and councillors. Keeping commitment to the proposal was essential with several low points when trustees believed that they were 'too small' to achieve a successful outcome and 'it was never going to happen'. Some felt unable to continue working with the project because association damaged external professional relationships with the local council. Prohibitive costs meant that the application would not be resubmitted if unsuccessful. With this insecurity, an additional concern was keeping parents who expressed strong interest involved. Nevertheless, support came from a well-established local school, providing the proposers with the confidence to proceed. This was perceived equally as valuable as the practical benefits of such 'strong external quality assurers'.

The problems outlined above further impinged on the issue of accommodation. If approval was finally given then school building funds would be available. Besides suitable indoor facilities, outdoor space was a regulatory requirement. The Council owned all potential sites and given their members' disapproval was explicitly only cooperating to their minimum legal obligation. The attendant uncertainty further provoked internal fears that parental support might prove unsustainable. These ultimately proved unfounded, partly due to proposers' tireless community engagement efforts and parents' dissatisfaction (across the locality's diverse ethnic mix) with alternative available schools.

### 4.1.3. Case 3 (School C)

*4.1.3.1. Proposer motivation and efforts.* This proposal, approved in July 2012, centred on a post heavy industrial area whose decline contributed to the area's perceived educational needs. The legacy of socially immobile families, alongside diminishing populations, had driven school consolidation with children having to travel further to attend. Families therefore long felt ignored regarding education. Reportedly, the highest spending local schools were the lowest performing so the issue lay in a shortage, not of school places, but perceived 'good' school places. Parents who were aware of the two 'good' schools in the area were willing to undertake time-consuming school runs across the city. Unsurprisingly, higher house prices near these schools militate against lower income home-owning families (alongside those in social housing) moving to the catchment areas. Local villagers expressing support for a Free School stimulated the proposal. The proposers formed a group of seven directors and seven occasional helpers with differing backgrounds (teacher, businessmen, accountant and architect) and with genuine altruistic motives. They intended that the school, while not faith-based, would have a Christian ethos. The proposers held six public meetings (generally in local pubs), distributed leaflets and made numerous phone calls. Sixty pupils per year will be admitted, the age ranging ultimately from 5 to 16. About 65 families pledged the school as their first choice. The reluctance from others to commit reportedly derived from the lack of a building.

*4.1.3.2. Support, opposition and process.* The DfE requirements were considered very demanding; long waiting periods for decisions exacerbating short required response times. Local responses were overwhelmingly positive, even from some teachers. Objections tended to be on ideological grounds, the LA opining a lack of need for another school. Other schools were opposed because of fear of falling pupil rolls.

### 4.1.4.   Case 4 (School D)

*4.1.4.1.   Proposer motivation and efforts.* The last case is a school based in a small town, consisting mainly of socio-economic C1 families. Nine local schools were described by the proposer as having 'diverse quality': with one recently in 'special measures' (a process for consistently underperforming schools as rated by the Government regulator, Ofsted). The rest did not exceed 'good' categorisation (one below the highest rating of 'outstanding'). Of the nine, two were oversubscribed, with some parents passing three schools to reach their preferred choice.

The proposer had run a nursery in the locality for many years, so setting up a Free School seemed a 'natural progression'. The proposers' ambitions for an 'outstanding' school entailed some pedagogical risk. Commensurate with the nursery's philosophy, the approach would centre on 'practical experiences' and 'hands on doing'. The proposer believed following DfE guidance 'tramlines' would not achieve beyond a 'good' Ofsted judgement. Thirty pupils per year would be admitted, meaning that full enrolment would eventually reach 210. While no preference would be given to current nursery children, most of the first year intake would have attended. Other admissions would be targeted at the several local (ex-mining) areas of deprivation.

Evidence of demand was generated from 3000 leaflets distributed in nearby estates. Five hundred parents were on a database with contact details and the school had an active Facebook page. This revealed a diversity of parents (mainly of professional backgrounds) all expressing dissatisfaction with their local school.

*4.1.4.2.   Support, opposition and process.* Opposition to the proposal came from local teachers, and local schools would not communicate; 'feelings were running quite high'. The views of councillors reflected conflicting political ideologies but they were pragmatic in recognising that 'the landscape was changing'.

The application process was described as 'horrendous'. The lack of financial help from the DfE was exacerbated by the expense of necessary days off work plus travel to London for meetings requiring overnight stays. The bureaucracy was 'very demanding' with 'no understanding of the manpower required'. Pupils were lost through the late DfE permission to open. The expense and personal sacrifice required by the application process was said to militate against proposals from the very deprived communities the policy was meant to serve. Some procedural elements were a 'nightmare', and to succeed proposers had to rely on much goodwill from local organisations.

## 4.2.   Research stage 2 – questionnaire findings

Questionnaire findings are presented here, tracing demand and motivation through to external support and opposition and application process experiences. In addition, perceptions on local parents' opinions and probable socio-economic backgrounds were separately explored (Table 1).

Eight primary schools, six secondary schools and four special/alternative schools and one 'all through' school sent questionnaire responses. Of these, 14 took pupils previously enrolled elsewhere while five did not.

Table 1. Free School Proposer Perspectives on Pupils' Families' Socio-Economic Background.

| Socio-economic group | % |
|---|---|
| AB Higher and intermediate managerial/administrative/professional | 14.2 |
| C1 Supervisory, clerical, junior managerial/administrative/professional | 32.8 |
| C2 Skilled manual workers | 13.6 |
| D Semi-skilled/unskilled manual workers | 19.3 |
| E On state benefit, unemployed, lowest grade workers | 20.0 |
| Total | 99.9 |

### 4.2.1. Demand and motivation

*4.2.1.1. Perceptions of demand.* Seven schools reported demand for places as roughly balanced with the supply with five undersubscribed and seven oversubscribed. Of those undersubscribed, one cited funding delays causing reduced demand, another *impending* school place shortages and another highlighted oversubscription for 2013–2014. If true, then 17 of the 19 could ordinarily predict adequate parental demand. If otherwise, this would drop to 14 of 19.

*4.2.1.2. Reactions from parents.* Regarding parent reactions (within the locality in general) prior to achieving Free School status, responses were overwhelmingly positive; 16 respondents reporting 'very supportive', the remaining three schools not reporting opposition. After Free School status was granted the position remained unchanged, indicating consistently strong support.

*4.2.1.3. Perceptions of socio-economic background.* Proposers' perceptions of socio-economic background of the pupils' families reflect the following crude averages:
While impossible to conduct tests of statistical significance, such responses suggest Free School applications *not* emanating from particular areas of socio-economic background, therefore suggesting diverse motivations behind opening Free Schools.

### 4.2.2. Proposer motivation

Beyond public mission statements, proposers were asked to rank various motivations for opening a Free School by importance. It was hoped to elicit frank expressions of principal motivation via this direct question, given guarantees of anonymity. The most common priority #1 response (seven of 19) was to improve 'the quality of education in a *less affluent* area', a ratio corresponding with applicant perceptions of future pupils' socio-economic classification, with 40% of pupils' families estimated to fit the D and E categories. Six priority #1 responses recorded 'a desire to establish a school with a different philosophy from those of schools in the area' with 'a perceived shortage of places' being the third most popular priority #1 response (with four recorded). These indicate concerns aligning with the Free School Policy's outward intentions; increasing quality, serving specific parent and pupil needs and fulfilling demand.
Regarding secondary motivations, 12 respondents offered further, evenly distributed reasons, three recorded in each of the following categories: 'a perceived

shortage of "good" school places', 'a desire to establish a school with a different philosophy from those of schools in the area', 'an inability of parents to have their children admitted to school of first choice' and 'to improve the quality of education in a less affluent area.'

Twenty-seven of the 55 schools opening in September 2012 were located in London (29%) or the South East (20%) where population growth may be putting pressure on school place supply.

### 4.2.3. Support and opposition

*4.2.3.1. Reactions from other schools.* In terms of reactions from other local schools while applying for Free School status, five of the 19 reported either 'opposed' or 'strongly opposed'. Two reported 'supportive' but most (12) replied 'neutral/mixed'.

When asked the nature of their opposition and/or support', responses varied. Since only seven of 19 responses returned 'opposed' or 'supportive', no generalisation is possible. However, the following comments exemplify the range of reactions, from adverse:

> Concerns that we would be taking students from them (other schools) (even though there are many unplaced children). We would be taking some of their funds. Not seeking to include the school in networks, supporting the local authority's opposition, twitter campaign by one affected school governor, telling parents the school would not open etc.

To mixed:

> Most of the local secondary schools were neutral as they were already heavily oversubscribed. Some primary schools very opposed and refused to distribute leaflets to year 6. Others supportive due to a science project we ran.

And in the particular case of one special school, constructive;

> Other special schools already worked with us and were supportive of the school expanding as children need the places.

Concerning other schools' reactions, subsequent to achieving Free School status, 12 respondents reported 'neutral/mixed'. Three schools previously either 'opposed', 'supportive' or 'very supportive' changed responses to 'neutral/mixed' while three schools previously 'neutral/mixed' became either 'very supportive' (two) or 'opposed', citing concern over impact on pupil numbers thus;

> Opposition intensified as we have taken many children (@200) from other schools.

Differences in reaction across other schools are illustrated as follows, perhaps indicating the criticality of individual school strategy-makers' perspectives on any perceived threat:

> Schools continue to feed negative messages to parents, though some have been more proactive in their own marketing which has been pleasing.

There were changes in reaction reported following DfE approval, with three deteriorating (becoming less supportive/more hostile), five improving and three remaining unchanged. Notwithstanding circumstantial nuances, it appears fear of competition (for pupils, staff and money) from the new school could be a significant factor. This was summarised by one respondent as 'fear of competition and fear of change'. Any support would come on pragmatic grounds. One school reported valuable assistance from a similar school beyond their region, illustrating that positive, long-distance relationships could occur.

*4.2.3.2. Reactions from LAs.* Political affiliation of LAs containing the surveyed Free School respondents and population is displayed in Table 2. Labour controlled over 60% of the total. There is no discernible sample bias.

Reactions to proposed Free Schools from LA officials and Councillors were enquired after. Most respondents (10) reported reactions 'opposed' or 'strongly opposed' although six responded 'supportive' or 'strongly supportive'. Surprisingly, origins of support and opposition, as political or personal, showed no obvious patterns at local level: a similar frequency of responses cited 'a political party' (Conservative supporting, Labour opposing), 'one or two councillors' and 'officials or others'. Two of the three 'special' or 'alternative provision' schools were in 'strongly supportive' Labour LAs. One (of three) Conservative LA was strongly opposed to the Free School in its constituency.

After schools were granted Free School status, reported reactions did change somewhat. Eight were 'neutral/mixed', six 'very supportive' or 'supportive' and two 'strongly opposed'. Reactions to 14 responders remained similar while five proposals reported improved reactions. None deteriorated.

A wide variety of related comments were given, including reports of openly hostile councils:

> The council still did everything they could to prevent us from opening and comments they made to the press did not help.

And

> It became clear that all avenues were being explored to scupper implementation, including through admissions processes and planning processes.

Contrasting enormously with sympathetic responses:

> Supportive from the outset.

Exemplifying the variety of Council reactions (reflecting the politically charged nature of Free Schools), one said that (more local) parish councillors were

Table 2. Political affiliation of controlling Local Authority of Free School.

| Political party | Labour | Conservative | Liberal Democrat | No over-all control | Unknown |
|---|---|---|---|---|---|
| Population | 33 | 12 | 0 | 10 | N/A |
| Respondents | 12 | 3 | 0 | 2 | 2 |

supportive while the borough council was opposed. Nevertheless, instances of officials recognising potential positive effects for pupils were noted;

An increased number of councillors saw the benefits to deprived children of the school.

Although political lines were broadly followed, an exception was reported; one Labour official strongly supporting a proposal, believing the new school would reduce social exclusion in the area.

*4.2.3.3.  Reactions from other sources.* On any noticeable reactions from other sources, there was evidence of strong local support from diverse origins, exemplified by these notable statements:

> ... over 1000 signatures from local residents. A third of these were from people who did not have children of the correct age to benefit from the school but could see the desperate need in the area. The local developers who plan 2500 houses for the local villages were also very supportive.

> Local organisations were very supportive. Felt that there was a need for a smaller school with explicit Christian ethos. Consultation approval was very high.

> Positive response from most local news providers. Press are very interested.

Nevertheless, in one instance antipathy originated *outside* the locality through existing schools' opposition to the policy, reflecting its controversial nature. These schools felt threatened despite no immediate impact on them.

> Schools outside our community have become more vocal in their opposition – they are concerned that the Free School programme might be expanded into their areas.

While not a representative sample, such responses do suggest a certain newsworthiness of Free Schools. Interest came from various perspectives, within and without their immediate location.

*4.2.4.  Application process*

Regarding the application process, 13 respondents reported it either 'extremely' or 'rather' bureaucratic, five 'about right' and none 'too lax' suggesting some dissatisfaction with the procedure. Perhaps given the reportedly 'onerous' nature of the process, strong and shared opinions were elicited, including concern over access to resources and capabilities:

> For groups without educational expertise it was extremely detailed and no money was provided to buy in consultancy ...

Multi-pronged criticism implying over-complexity and lack of proposer control:

> Helpful to have a DfE project officer. Too many lawyers. Awful system for pre-opening finance. (We had n)o control over use of funding for project management.

And an unreliable, difficult and detached system:

The process was however a nightmare in many ways – a tick box process that was constantly changing – n.b. particularly the financial elements.

As well as downright exasperation:

A botched job from beginning to end!

However, from the respondents suggesting the process was 'about right', came recognition of thoroughness being important regarding schools:

The process was rigorous but absolutely correct. One would expect rigour when applying to secure such a significant project for young people.

And Government money:

Any process that involves committing tax payers' money over a lengthy period must necessarily involve checks and bureaucracy. The key thing is to have a lead at the DfE who is readily available to help answer questions.

However, while rigour was appreciated (as above), timely, consistent and practical support would have been helpful.

When asked about process improvements, bureaucratic overburdening was a theme, unsurprising since most proposers could not work full time on it. In the four mini-cases, two proposers were already running a school; the remaining two employed elsewhere. While distaste for bureaucracy could cause concern given the administrative requirements of schools, it is unlikely that proposers would run the schools themselves; full-time staff would be employed for such tasks.

Accordingly, given the majority view of a bureaucratic process, some respondents suggested reducing the 'number of copies of memorandums, documents etc.' alongside improving and fixing application milestone deadlines. The consequences of unreliable timescales were outlined thus:

(T)he delay signing the funding agreement … meant … a number of parents started to worry that we would not open and we lost children.

This echoed other respondents' calls for the DfE to meet *its* deadlines and respond promptly to emails.

The cost of the application process was often mentioned; suggestions included a standard grant or fixed budget for setting up rather than a negotiated sum. One respondent applying for the second time said:

I very much liked the old process where proposer groups created a 30 page document and were then provided funds to further specify the school.

A couple of respondents desired more trust from the DfE, although taxpayers might prefer trust to be earned throughout a transparent process. Some reservations also existed over training quality from DfE project leads.

### 4.2.5. New schools network

Regarding the NSN's role, 12 respondents reported it 'helpful' or 'very helpful', four 'neutral' and two 'unhelpful' or 'very unhelpful'. Such distribution of responses reflects generally positive feedback with reservations, exemplified positively:

> (w)e could not have done this without the NSN; they provided so much knowledge and advice.

And ambivalently:

> (t)hey were pretty much irrelevant – a couple of entertaining afternoon teas but no help.

Appreciation to a point was reflected:

> Good advice initially on the application but procedural rather than qualitative (or financial). Understandably they won't advise in any meaningful way.

Nevertheless, the simple existence of support could be helpful:

> Reviewing our bid, being at the end of the phone to consult, supporting us prior to interview.

Especially representing groups in front of the DfE:

> A loud voice with those who matter when prompt decisions are needed. Disadvantage is London centric location.

Limitations of the Capital base struck a chord elsewhere:

> The meeting in London was costly and unnecessary.

While the Capital focus seems a necessary trade-off for achieving a 'loud voice' with Central Government, regional Free School proposers would have appreciated some accommodation of their needs.
One response indicated potential irrelevance where other institutions assisted:

> The NSN is a splendid catalyst but (another education institution) has substantially more experience than the network and it (NSN) has been fairly marginal as a result.

## 5. Discussion

Analysis of emerging themes follows by research stage.

### 5.1. Discussion of interview findings

#### 5.1.1. Proposer motivation

Internally, motivation to improve education where quality was lacking was common throughout. School A reflected concern to *maintain* good teaching and learning practice, by supporting the organisation's continued existence (and associated employment) in trying economic times. Therefore, refocusing on the nearby lower income community would be mutually beneficial. Schools C and D were more clearly focused on educational *improvement*, although the poor socio-economic backgrounds made the need pressing. However, actual backgrounds of families signing up, despite relatively deprived school locations, were uncertain. Founders' pro-active awareness-raising efforts built on reportedly existing desires for local education quality improvement. School B proposers gauged needs via a long-standing community commitment, recognising (against the Council view) the criticality of innovative new ventures for tackling perceived persistent educational failure. In all cases, some level of altruism was said to combine with intentions to address local demand for improved education.

### 5.1.2. Experience of process, support and opposition

There were significant commonalities across experiences of the application process. External ideological and/or political opposition contrasted reported overwhelmingly positive parental responses. Practically, there were common opinions regarding a confused, bureaucratic and expensive process, combined with difficulties in securing school premises, meaning significant resilience and commitment to overcoming challenge was required.

Important social justice issues arise when considering opposition. The Local Authority is expected to ensure good-quality education for all children, not just those of 'pushy parents'. While LA resistance to losing educational control and existing schools' fear of competition might be understandable to this extent, it is questionable whether these reactions ultimately had individual pupil learning and welfare at heart given the disparity with parental wishes. Some Local Authority perspectives may originate in social justice perceptions favouring structured solutions to equalising educational opportunities for all their pupils that are potentially indirectly affected by single 'disruptive' schools. However, opposition was not necessarily outwardly manifested: the more flexible, pragmatic attitudes related by School D proposers contrasting School B's difficult experiences.

## 5.2. Discussion of questionnaire findings

The 19 of 55 potential respondents further illustrated patterns in motivation, experiences and support/opposition.

### 5.2.1. Proposer motivation

Diverse motivations were uncovered, although all responded to some identified local demand. Issues of scarcity and lack of educational quality were emphasised as much as providing for children of deprived backgrounds. Therefore, proposer responses at least suggest accordance with the policy's stated intentions for improving education for disadvantaged communities. This was expected given that all respondents were successful.

### 5.2.2. Experience of process, support and opposition

As above, it is interesting comparing the generally positive parental response to proposed Free Schools – they have the most interest and commitment to their children's future – with ideological or party political opposition or based on other schools' fear of competition for resources and change. Given respondents' success in starting Free Schools it was predictable they would report support and demand for their school, as an application process prerequisite. However, the reported general lack of dissenting voices among parents, if true, powerfully indicates ground-level feeling where concern lies rather with pressing and personal educational issues. Importantly, this study takes its information from Free School proposers' views on all parents' opinions, not just those sending pupils to the school. Some proposers explicitly highlighted positive reactions of other parents.

Contrast between political opposition and parental support neatly frames the ideological and philosophical debate surrounding positioning of responsibility for schooling and education. Justifications for antipathy towards parental choice in education beyond special interest can lie in transcendental views on social justice prioritising ideal institutional and societal structures over their practical consequences, experienced more keenly at individual level.

From this ground-level perspective, ensuring new Free Schools fulfil parent and pupil needs for educational quality, a demanding process to demonstrate fitness to set up these new institutions is desirable. However, a mechanistic administrative system is no substitute for effective and efficient application processes. An inconsistent and expensive process also militates against applications from poorer/more socially deprived elements of society especially given scarce time, resources and capabilities. Shifting measurements and delayed Government responses caused significant additional problems to successful applications, compounded by external opposition. Increased transparency of selection criteria and consistency of process would have reduced unnecessary expense, greatly benefitting the Free School proposers and ultimately the policy. Perceived box-ticking exercises deflecting genuine efforts to identify and meet demand, combined with adverse campaigns, could leave some demand unrealised for (understandably) cautious parents.

Difficulties in accessing suitable buildings exacerbated this, especially where cooperation was minimal from influential local Councils. Vital to inspiring demand, buildings represented an important physical symbol for parents concerned with their children's education. Responses suggest that this aspect required revisiting to facilitate success for worthy applications. Without alternative solutions, this key sticking point could hamper the policy achieving the scale envisaged by UK Government.

Assistance from the NSN was valued by many applicants. Support of other experienced schools and educational organisations were greatly appreciated where available. Given likely minimal assistance for future applicants from some local Councils, facilitating a system of support networks and forums could enable appropriate, relevant advice. Similar proposals likely exist across regions, *and* intra-regional assistance could be useful within specific area circumstances. A 'buddy' system or Skype networks could, for example, be easily organised. Genuine Free School proposals based on laudable motives, meeting local educational demand, could then source required expertise from sympathetic process 'veterans'. Furthermore, means of supplying some initial finance could facilitate larger scale success for worthy but resource-strapped, ground-level proposals. Subsequently providing access to support and mentoring from previously successful Free School applicants and networking opportunities between current applicants, the NSN has broached this strategy. However, the Development Programme is limited in reach and future research might evaluate its effectiveness.

## 6. Conclusion

This study has produced responses largely appearing to fulfil the Free Schools' philosophical objectives, allowing organisations to set up demand-driven schools. Limited access to necessary resources and expertise and overreliance on central bureaucracy could stall the process. The recent DfE application alterations encouraging accelerated replication of successful models and engendering support among Free School groups are important for enabling transformative educational effects at significant scale. Regarding individual groups' efforts, the four schools interviewed all demonstrated substantive efforts to consult local families in perceived catchment areas. These indicated strong local support for the proposed schools. Questionnaire responses indicated varied motivations for opening a Free School. However, three motives seemed to take precedence:

improving 'the quality of education in less affluent area'

'a desire to establish a school with a different philosophy from those schools in the area' and

rectifying 'a perceived shortage of places'.

Free School proposers found, perhaps unsurprisingly, opposition from 'threatened' existing schools and local politicians and officials, philosophical in origin.

Despite Coalition website claims that setting up schools is now easier for 'teachers, charities, parents and education experts' (DfE 2013a), most proposers found the application process overly demanding, inconsistent and bureaucratic. While scrutiny is justified when allocating tax funds for educating children, responses here suggest a costly, confused process for resource-strapped, time-poor applicants, subject to incremental changes. Unless this, and funding and buildings issues are resolved, ground-level attempts to meet educational demand and the scheme's sustainable impact may be compromised. Certainty, transparency and standardisation should be minimum procedural requirements for identifying valid and worthy applications. There is hope that recent adaption of policy implementation can facilitate this.

Most respondents highlighted the NSN as a helpful source of advice and encouragement. However, widely accessible networks of schools and 'buddy' systems might enhance the reach, timeliness and specificity of advice, building on valuable procedural experience resources, better serving large numbers of applications while supporting fledgling proposals with trying local circumstances.

Given Free Schools' ideological climate, comprehensive research into their impacts on pupil and communities is advocated, for analysis and subsequent enhancement, beyond any agenda. Rigorous impact evaluations contrasting educational progress in children at Free Schools with peers in surrounding communities and across areas with and without Free Schools would enlighten debate at a practical level concerning the effects of these 'additional schools' on *overall* quality and equality. Instigating this early would provide a strong base for policy development.

Beyond immediately measurable impact, opening up education further to diverse providers under proper scrutiny could allow a scaling up of promising innovations benefiting pupils outside discrete localities. Learning organisations implementing best practice could then grow. Greater emphasis on parental desires could then simplify the application process, re-rooting the policy in ground level accountability. A more open system could allow pro-active, specialised schools to serve those unwilling or unable to make educational choices for their children. In the meantime, the considerable efforts of proposers seeking to meet parental demand for their children's education should be supported with access to resources and expertise, tailored to their needs. Groups proving themselves adept at improving community education should be encouraged to expand their work to locations where educational quality is similarly needed and desired.

Finally, one should recognise the Free Schools initiative as being in its infancy. Initial new Free Schools may not represent subsequent ventures, in their character, structure (school chains may form) and success. The initiative will be threatened by reactions to Free School failures (some are inevitable) and possible changes of Government, not least in 2015. As (and if) the policy matures, evaluation of social justice effects at the education system level will be possible, depending on the differing criteria for perceived realisation, rooted in conflicting philosophical traditions. While debate continues at that elevated level, parents and pupils are entitled to seek out and create their preferred educational pathways, supported by willing providers.

## References

Academies Act. 2010. c. 32 (Eng.).
Allen, R., and S. Burgess. 2011a. "Open Public Services: How do the White Paper's Five Principles Apply to Schools?" *Research in Public Policy* 13: 7–8.
Allen, R., and S. Burgess. 2011b. "Free Schools: What are they Good for? Public Finance." http://opinion.publicfinance.co.uk/2011/09/free-schools-what-are-they-good-for/.
Ball, S. J. 2012. "The Reluctant State and the Beginning of the End of State Education." *Journal of Educational Administration and History* 44 (2): 89–103.

Bergstrom, B. 2012. "The Story of a School Entrepreneur." In *The Profit Motive in Education: Continuing the Revolution*, edited by J. Stanfield, 86–95. London: Institute of Economic Affairs.

Buchanan, J. M. 2003. "Public Choice: Politics without Romance." *Policy* 19 (3): 13–18.

Bush, T. 1995. *Theories of Educational Management*. London: Paul Chapman Publishing.

Chapman, C., and M. Salokangas. 2012. "Independent State-funded Schools: Some Reflections on Recent Developments." *School Leadership & Management: Formerly School Organisation* 32 (5): 473–486.

Conservative Party. "New Free Schools set to Open." http://www.conservatives.com/News/News_stories/2011/09/New_Free_Schools_set_to_open.aspx.

Croft, J. 2011. *Profit-making Free Schools*. London: Adam Smith Research Trust.

DfE (Department for Education). 2010. "The Importance of Teaching. The Schools White Paper." http://www.official-documents.gov.uk/.

DfE (Department for Education). 2012. "Free Schools in 2014 How to Apply." https://www.gov.uk/government/publications/free-schools-in-2014-how-to-apply-mainstream-and-16-to-19-free-schools.

DfE (Department for Education). 2013a. "Free Schools." http://www.education.gov.uk/schools/leadership/typesofschools/freeschools.

DfE (Department for Education). 2013b. "Free Schools Opening in 2013 and beyond Admissions – FAQs." http://media.education.gov.uk/assets/files/pdf/f/admissions%20faqs%20v2.pdf.

DfE (Department for Education). 2013c. "Free Schools: How to Apply." http://media.education.gov.uk/assets/files/pdf/f/free%20school%20how%20to%20apply%20guide.pdf.

Hatcher, R. 2011. "The Conservative-liberal Democrat Coalition government's 'Free Schools' in England." *Educational Review* 63 (4): 485–503.

Hultin, A. 2012. "Why is There no IKEA in Education?" In *The Profit Motive in Education: Continuing the Revolution*, edited by J. Stanfield, 143–155. London: Institute of Economic Affairs.

NSN (New Schools Network). http://newschoolsnetwork.org/.

Power, S., and C. Taylor. 2013. "Social Justice and Education in the Public and Private Spheres." *Oxford Review of Education* 39 (4): 533–547.

Rawls, J. 1971. *A Theory of Justice*. Cambridge, MA: Harvard University Press.

Schein, E. H. 2010. *Organizational Culture and Leadership*. Hoboken: Wiley.

Sen, A. 2009. *The Idea of Justice*. London: Allen Lane.

Sergiovanni, T. J. 2003. "The Lifeworld at the Center: Values and Action in Educational Leadership." In *Effective Educational Leadership*, edited by N. Bennett, M. Crawford, and M. Cartwright, 14–24. London: Paul Chapman Publishing.

Stanfield, J. 2012. "Profit in Education – Not a Dirty Word." Institute of Directors Big Picture, Winter. http://www.iod.com/~/media/Documents/PDFs/Influencing/Big%20Picture/BP%202012/profitineducationnotadirtyworddec12.pdf.

Tooley, J. 2000. *Reclaiming Education*. London: Cassell.

Tooley, J. 2013. "Challenging Educational Injustice: 'Grassroots' Privatisation in South Asia and Sub-Saharan Africa." *Oxford Review of Education* 39 (4): 533–547.

Walford, G. 2000. "From City Technology Colleges to Sponsored Grant-Maintained Schools." *Oxford Review of Education* 26 (2): 145–158.

Walford, G. 2006. *Markets and Equity in Education*. London: Continuum.

Whitty, G., and S. Power. 2000. "Marketization and Privatization in Mass Education Systems." *International Journal of Educational Development* 20: 93–107.

Wright, A. 2012. "Fantasies of Empowerment: Mapping Neoliberal Discourse in the Coalition government's Schools Policy." *Journal of Education Policy* 27 (3): 279–294.

Young, T. 2012. "Setting up a Free School." In *The Profit Motive in Education: Continuing the Revolution*, edited by J. Stanfield, 61–73. London: Institute of Economic Affairs.

# Index

Absolute Return for Kids (ARK) 75
Academies: chains 2, 33, 48, 61–2, 75, 92, 108; choice of schools 24, 39, 44, 68–70, 74, 77, 80; Coalition Government 1–2, 25, 40, 64; converter schools 1–3, 9–11, 19, 24–5, 41–50, 75, 78–82; failing schools, replacement of 1–2, 60–1, 63; fees, inability to charge 2, 61, 75; free school meals (FSMs) eligible pupils 7–12, 15–19, 78, 80; funding 1, 2, 7, 24, 60, 65; new schools 1–2, 7, 24–34, 40, 60–3; numbers 1–2, 7, 60–2, 75; opposition 25, 29–30, 42–3; primary schools, extension to 2, 11–12, 24, 61, 74–5; profit motive 42, 50, 61, 69–71, 73, 75, 81; religious schools 24–6, 60–1, 75–6; secondary schools 2, 7, 11; social justice 1, 3, 7, 19, 24, 63; socio-economic status (SES) segregation 3, 7, 11–19, 24, 80; special schools, extension to 2, 61; sponsors/sponsorship 1, 3, 7, 11–12, 24–5, 33, 41, 60, 63–4, 74–6; successful schools, conversion of 1–2, 4, 40, 60–1; teachers' salaries scales and terms of employment 1–2, 61, 65; Technical Academies 40 *see also* Free Schools; joint church Academies; politics of Academies Programme; pupil intakes to academies and attainment
Academies Act 2010 1–2, 5, 44, 75, 79, 89, 95
Academies Enterprise Trust (AET) 75
access to school/admissions 77–82: common application forms 78; equal opportunities 5, 69–70; Free Schools 63, 90, 96, 98; joint church Academies 29; oversubscription criteria 78–9; policy goals and development 74, 75; religious schools 29, 70; School Admissions Code 78–9; Sweden, *Friskolor* in 77–8, 81
accountability: Academies 38–9, 45; democratic accountability 25; Free Schools 65, 90, 107; philanthropists and business people, participation of 25; policy goals and development since 1980s 74, 75
admissions *see* access to school/admissions
Adonis, Andrew 50

age range 9, 11–12, 19–20, 89, 97
*Ambitions for Britain* manifesto (New Labour) 39
Andersson, Eva 79–80
Annual Schools Census (ASC) 3, 7, 8
Anti-Academies Alliance 42
Apple, Michael W 45
Arendt, Hannah 4, 39, 46–50
Arreman, Inger Erixon 77
Assisted Places 63
attainment *see* pupil intakes to academies and attainment
autonomy of schools 44, 55, 68, 70, 74, 82

*Back Papers on Education* 57
Baker, Kenneth 56, 57–8
Ball, Stephen J 25, 29, 92
behavioural difficulties, children diagnosed with 8
birth-rate, growth in 2, 62
Blair, Tony 1, 41, 60–1
Blunkett, David 39, 41, 60
Board of Governors, degree of control of 54
Böhlmark, Anders 79
Bourdieu, Pierre 28, 30–1
British Academy (BA) 42
Buchanan, James M 93
Business Academy Bexley 9–10, 16–19

Carlisle, Mark 57
catchment areas 12, 29, 62, 96–7, 107
Centre for Policy Studies (CPS) 57
Chadwick, Priscilla 24, 26, 28, 31–2, 34–5
chains of schools 2, 33, 48, 61–2, 75, 92, 108
Chapman, Christopher 92
charitable trusts 53, 56, 92
charity schools 2, 4, 53–6, 58, 61–2, 75, 92, 96, 107
children, rights of 24
Chitty, Clyde 60
choice of schools: Academies 24, 39, 44, 68–70, 74, 77, 80; City Technology Colleges (CTCs) 56–7; Free Schools 90, 92–4, 97–8, 100, 106, 108; grant-maintained schools 58;

# INDEX